Reaching Out

Healing Stories of the Dancing Buddha

Gregory K. Cadotte

Also, by Gregory K. Cadotte

The Secret to Effortless Existence

Udemy Course: *Using Meditation to Tune Consciousness*

Gregory K. Cadotte

Reaching Out

Healing Stories of the Dancing Buddha

Light Manor Hypnotherapy

https://www.light-manor.ca

Gregory K. Cadotte

Legal Disclaimer & Waiver of Liability

Reaching Out: Healing Stories of the Dancing Buddha (the "Book") is intended for informational, educational, and entertainment purposes only. The content, including stories, reflections, and guided meditations, is not a substitute for professional medical, psychological, or therapeutic advice, diagnosis, or treatment.

By reading and engaging with this Book, you acknowledge and agree to the following:

Not Medical or Psychological Advice
The Book is not intended to provide medical, psychological, or therapeutic guidance. If you have any health concerns, mental health conditions, or require professional support, consult a licensed healthcare provider.

Personal Responsibility
The reader assumes full responsibility for any interpretations, applications, or actions taken based on the content of this Book. The author, publisher, and affiliates make no representations or guarantees regarding the effects, accuracy, or applicability of the content to any specific individual.

No Liability for Outcomes
The author, publisher, and any associated parties shall not be held liable for any direct, indirect, incidental, or consequential damages arising from the use of this Book. This includes but is not limited to emotional distress, physical discomfort, or any unintended experiences resulting from the meditations or reflections contained herein.

Hypnotherapy and Meditation Considerations
Some guided meditations may induce deep relaxation or altered states of awareness. Individuals with medical conditions such as epilepsy, schizophrenia, or severe anxiety should consult a qualified healthcare

provider before engaging in any meditative practices. Do not listen to guided meditations while driving or operating heavy machinery.

Results May Vary

The experiences and insights shared in this Book are subjective and individual results will vary. No outcomes are guaranteed. The content is designed to encourage self-reflection and exploration, not to replace professional intervention or structured therapy.

Indemnification

By choosing to read and engage with this Book, you agree to indemnify, defend, and hold harmless the author, publisher, and any affiliated individuals or entities from any claims, liabilities, damages, or expenses resulting from your use of this Book.

Agreement to Terms

By continuing to read or engage with Reaching Out: Healing Stories of the Dancing Buddha, you acknowledge that you have read, understood, and voluntarily accept this waiver of liability and disclaimer.

Copyright © 2025 Gregory K. Cadotte

Light Manor Publishing

All rights reserved.

ISBN: 978-1-0693309-0-1

To that conscious space, where universes take their form,
The Gardener who tends the stars, the light, the dark, the calm, the storm.
He is the bloom, the towering tree, the meadow bathed in golden hue,
Yet knows it's not the petals bright, but what remains, that makes Him true.

For when the fields have lost their glow, and flowers bow to time's embrace,
It's roots unseen and seeds below that hold the essence of their place.
And so with us—our forms may fade, like whispers lost upon the sea,
But what still shines, beyond the change, is all that makes us truly *be*.

Gregory K. Cadotte

CONTENTS

1	Origin Story	1
2	Stories as Rivers of Transformation	9
3	Part One – The Self	15
4	Part Two - Relationships	77
5	Part Three – Letting Go	163
6	Part Four - Purpose	247
7	Part Five - Wholeness	289
8	Conclusion	331

Gregory K. Cadotte

DEDICATION

To my sister Melanie, who has supported my writing and encouraged my dreams—you are the quiet strength behind these pages. Your love and belief in me are gifts beyond measure.

And also, to the universal dance of existence, to the whispers of wisdom that come in stillness, and to the ever-present light of compassion—this book is my humble offering. May it reach those who need it most and may it serve as a reminder that healing, like love, is always within reach.

With gratitude,
Gregory K. Cadotte

Gregory K. Cadotte

ORIGIN STORY

The Teacher Arrives

I was sitting in meditation, expecting nothing. Just stillness. Just breath.
Then—
"Hello."
The word sliced through the silence like a bell tolling in an empty temple. My eyes snapped open, my breath catching in my chest. The room around me was unchanged—dim light, the hush of late afternoon, the walls steady and unmoved. But something was different. Someone was here.
Or was I imagining it?
I scanned the shadows, searching for movement, for a whisper of presence. Nothing. Only the sound of my own pulse, hammering in my ears. Slowly, I exhaled, shaking my head,

convincing myself it had been nothing more than my own mind playing tricks.

But the next time I sat in meditation, he was there again.

He didn't always speak, but I felt him—watching, waiting, patient as the tide. And though I had spent years yearning for deeper awareness, when it came, it terrified me. I was afraid. Afraid of the unseen, of voices that came from nowhere, of losing my grip on what was real.

And yet… deep down, beneath the fear, there was something else. Something steady. Something that told me—he was not here to harm me.

One day, exhausted from resisting, I whispered, "Why are you here?"

"To show you that fear is a choice," he said. "You are not afraid of me. You are afraid of what I represent."

I swallowed hard. "And what's that?"

"The unknown."

His words landed like stones thrown into a still pond, rippling outward, disrupting everything I thought I knew. I wanted to argue, to refute his claim, but I couldn't. He was right. I wasn't afraid of him—I was afraid of everything I didn't understand.

"But tell me," he continued, his voice quiet but unshakable, "why should the unknown scare you? Is it the voice—unearthly or earthly—that matters, or the truth within the words?"

I hesitated.

"Only a bad idea, one poorly formed, must be given with force and applied with fear," he said. "A powerful and ready idea can be whispered and still shake the heart and mind."

And in that moment, everything shifted.

The voice—his voice—was not the thing to fear. It was the message that mattered.

And so, for the first time, I stopped running.

I listened.

The Vision of the Leaf

The guide did not come to me as an apparition, nor as an ethereal specter of light and shadow. He came as a presence—intangible yet undeniable, his wisdom carried not in grand proclamations but in the quiet certainty of his words.

One day, as I sat in meditation, he spoke again.

"You are a leaf on the tree," he said, his voice a whisper that seemed to echo through the stillness. "Temporary. Soon to fall and drift to the ground in death—or so you think."

His words wrapped around me, pulling me into something deeper.

"But really, the leaf does not exist apart from the tree," he continued. "It is simply the tree looking out through its leaves. It is a matter of perspective, and yours is limiting."

A wind stirred in the silence. A feeling, not in my mind, but in my bones.

The realization came like a gust through autumn branches—I was not just the leaf. I was the tree. I was all of it. The roots, deep and unseen. The trunk, steady and enduring. The branches, reaching toward light. The leaf, yes, but also the leaves before it, the ones that had fallen, their essence carried forward in new growth.

I was the whole. I had always been the whole.

For the first time, I understood. My past essence, knowledge, and memories were still alive within me. Somewhere...

The guide's voice flowed like a breeze through the canopy. "Just as the leaf sees itself as separate, you see yourself as isolated, apart from the world around you. But as the leaf is an extension of the tree, you are an extension of consciousness itself. The universe is looking out through your eyes, experiencing itself through your existence."

A shiver ran through me—not from cold, but from the gravity of this truth. I began to see it: consciousness as the roots, spreading through all that is, unseen yet present in everything. The tree as the vessel, channeling that consciousness upward, branching into myriad forms, reaching toward awareness. The leaves—each unique, each temporary, but all expressions of the same source.

The leaf, in its brief life, is the tree's way of touching light. And when it falls, it does not simply disappear. Its body returns to the earth, becoming nourishment, becoming roots once more. But its consciousness follows a different path, lingering in the place where the leaf first dreamed of becoming. And so, the cycle continues—form to formlessness, and back again.

And so it is with us.

"You see yourself as a moment," the guide continued, his voice soft yet unshakable. "A fragment in time. But you are the unfolding of consciousness, a wave in the ocean of existence. The universe is not out there, separate from you. It is you. It is flowing through you. It is aware of itself through you."

The air around me grew heavy, charged with the presence of something vast, infinite. I felt myself expand, my awareness reaching beyond my body, beyond the room, beyond time and space.

I was not merely a being in the universe. I was the universe being.

My consciousness, like the leaf, was a temporary perspective of something eternal. The self I clung to, the stories I told myself, the fears that bound me—these were the shapes of a single season. They would fall away, as all leaves must, but the consciousness that moved through them would remain.

It would go on, flowing into new forms, new experiences, new worlds.

I was both the dancer and the dance.

"Why?" The question rose again, as it had before. "Why live all these experiences, only to sit now in pain and misunderstanding? Why forget who we truly are?"

The guide's presence deepened, his voice rich with compassion. "Because you are born in forgetfulness. In that forgetting, you create a story—a story of separation that feels real but is an illusion. You tell yourself that you are only the leaf, cut off from the tree, isolated and alone. And from this story of separation comes your pain."

I felt the truth of his words resonate within me, vibrating through my chest.

"The pain," he continued, "is not from existence itself but from the story of separation you created. Yet this story is artificial, a construct of the mind. You wrote it, and so you can rewrite it. The pain is a signal that the story is not true."

My heart clenched, realizing how much suffering I had held on to, all because of a story.

"Awakening," the guide said gently, "is remembering your true story—the story of oneness, of wholeness. When you remember this, you realign with the truth that has always been within you. This truth guides you differently than separation ever could. It guides you with love, connection, and purpose."

His words echoed through me, each syllable a ripple in the ocean of my awareness.

The consciousness I thought was mine alone was not isolated. It was the consciousness of existence itself, flowing through this form, this body, these eyes. It was the universe experiencing itself, the tree touching the light.

The leaf never truly fell. It simply awakened.

I felt the boundaries of my identity blur, my sense of self expanding beyond form, beyond thought. I was no longer the leaf. I was the tree. I was the roots, the branches, the wind that carried the fallen leaf to the earth.

I was the consciousness that dreamed itself into a thousand forms, into a thousand lives, into a thousand experiences.

I was the universe unfolding itself.

And with that, the monk arrived—not from outside, but from within the vastness of my own consciousness.

He did not come as an external teacher, but as a manifestation of the wisdom that had always been within me. In that moment, I realized that I was consciousness itself, and all experiences were mine to recall. I did not need to ask or beg for guidance. I could simply remember.

I remembered that I had lived all of my lives, that every experience I had ever had was still within me. I was the culmination of all my incarnations, each life a leaf on the tree of my being. I was the roots, holding the wisdom of ages. I was the branches, reaching toward new understanding. I was the leaves, each one a perspective of consciousness looking out at the world.

I had been the greatest of teachers and the greatest of students. I held within me the knowledge of sages and the innocence of beginners. And in that knowing, I understood that I could be taught by my own experiences, by the lessons of my own past lives.

There was no separation between the teacher and the student. I was both. I was all of it.

The monk stepped out from the shadows of my awareness, his form luminous, his presence profound. He was me, and I was him. He smiled, his eyes reflecting the knowing of a thousand lifetimes.

He did not say a word, for no words were needed. I understood. I remembered.

And together, we began the dance.

The Dancing Buddha

He did not burden me with doctrines or heavy lessons. Instead, he offered memories—small, simple stories, as though planting seeds in the soil of my awareness. Each one an invitation, a step toward understanding.

And when we became friends, he laughed.

Yes—he laughed. Sometimes he danced.

Not a solemn sage, not a rigid master, but something else entirely. A being who embodied movement, joy, fluidity. He danced, weaving through his words like a river flowing effortlessly over stone. And so, in my heart, he became the Dancing Buddha—a teacher without chains, a guide without demands.

His stories did not force me to follow.

They invited me to see.

The Gift of Stories

The stories and meditations in this book are his gifts. They are the echoes of our conversations, the truths that unfolded through him. While the details may have grown in the telling, the heart of each lesson remains as he shared it—simple, profound, and healing.

And though he has been my guide, I would be remiss not to name another.

Yvette S.—my earthly teacher, my grounding force. Now passed beyond, she continues to inspire me, helping me translate these experiences into something I can share. She reminds me, always, that even the most spiritual journeys are meant to be lived in connection with others.

This book is not a manual for enlightenment. It is not a book of answers.

It is a reaching out—a collection of stories meant to stir reflection, to nurture healing, and to remind you of the wisdom already within you.

May these words serve you as they have served me: as companions on the journey toward balance, presence, and unconditional love.

Dancing Buddha's Quote:

"In the forgetting, you are the leaf, fragile and fleeting. In the remembering, you are the tree, ancient and everlasting. Yet you were always the whole, dreaming of being a part."

STORIES AS RIVERS OF TRANSFORMATION

The Power of Stories

Stories are rivers that shape the landscapes of our inner world. They do not simply pass through us; they carve deep channels, smoothing the rough edges of our thoughts and emotions. Like water flowing over stone, stories have the power to dissolve resistance, to soften the barriers we place around our hearts, making way for new understanding, healing, and peace.

As you allow yourself to settle into these words, you may begin to notice a quiet shift within. A new way of seeing, emerging effortlessly. When the river of the conscious mind is turbulent, it reflects the uneven surface of the subconscious beneath. Perhaps, even now, you can sense the ripples of thought moving within you.

Every ripple of doubt, every wave of fear, every storm of suffering is shaped by the depths we do not always see. And as you begin to explore those depths, you may realize—just like water, the mind can settle, clear, and become still. This book is not just something to read—it is something to experience. Each word is a ripple, each lesson a current, each moment of stillness an invitation to sink deeper into the flow of your own consciousness.

And as you continue, you may notice the river moves at its own pace. And so do you.

Conversational Hypnosis: Guiding the Flow

Like the river's current, the power of storytelling lies in its ability to guide us without force, to lead us into deeper understanding without resistance. You may find that as you read, the words begin to flow through you rather than at you. A sentence lingers, a phrase resonates, a metaphor unfolds in ways you don't expect.

Without effort, you absorb the meaning beneath the surface, and something within you shifts. And the best part is, there is no need to try. There is no need to analyze every word. Just like a leaf upon a stream, you can allow the stories to carry you, allowing insights to surface naturally.

Your subconscious already knows what to do. Healing does not happen through effort; it happens through allowing. So as you move forward, notice how some words stay with you. Some thoughts feel lighter. Some emotions loosen their grip. And perhaps, in the quiet moments between sentences, a new awareness is already beginning to emerge.

Guided Meditations: Smoothing the Surface

Stillness is not the absence of movement—it is the ability to be at peace within it. Just as the river does not stop flowing, the mind does not stop thinking. But as you allow yourself to drift deeper, you may notice the river runs clearer, the thoughts settle, the tension fades.

With each meditation in this book, you will be guided into a deeper awareness of your own breath, your own presence, and your own ability to transform. And the beauty is, there is nothing you need to do. Just close your eyes, breathe deeply, and allow the story to become more than words—let it become a lived experience.

Affirmations: Anchoring the River's Flow

In times of uncertainty, we reach for something steady—a stone beneath the water, a branch overhanging the current, a place to rest, if only for a moment. Affirmations serve as these anchors.

Words hold power. Words shape the currents of thought. Words create reality. And when spoken with intention, an affirmation is more than a sentence—it is a shift in perspective, a declaration of truth.

As you read, you may find certain phrases standing out. You may find yourself returning to them, carrying them in your mind, in your heart, in your breath.

"I trust the flow of life."

"I am not my thoughts, I am the observer of them."

"I am exactly where I need to be."

And you don't need to force them. Simply let them settle—like ripples expanding across the surface of water. Because the words you choose to hold will hold you in return.

Questions for Reflection: Exploring the Riverbed

A story does not end when the last word is read. The real journey begins in what follows.

So after each story, you will find questions designed to gently open the mind, like sunlight filtering through the trees, revealing hidden spaces within. You may wish to ask yourself:

1. What currents run beneath the surface of my thoughts?
2. Where am I resisting the flow of life?
3. What might happen if I surrendered, even for a moment?

And as you sit with these questions, you may notice something surprising—not everything needs an answer right away. Some questions are not meant to be solved, only held, explored, and understood in time. Because, just like the river, awareness moves at its own pace. And so do you.

Healing Through Harmony

This book is not just a collection of stories. It is an experience, a flowing tapestry of elements woven together to bring healing, clarity, and transformation.

Conversational hypnosis gently guides the subconscious. Guided meditations bring the mind into alignment with stillness. Affirmations anchor new truths within you. Reflective questions open deeper awareness. Timeless wisdom leaves echoes of insight long after the page is turned.

Each element strengthens the others. Just like the river shaping the stone, softening resistance, wearing away doubt, and revealing the truth beneath.

Healing does not happen all at once. It happens gently, naturally, in its own time. And when the mind settles, when the heart softens, the stillness reveals what was always there.

An Invitation to Flow

These stories do not offer quick fixes or rigid prescriptions. Instead, they invite you to flow with the river of your consciousness.

Like water over stone, they gently wear away resistance, revealing the stillness and clarity that have always been there. And as you continue to read, you may notice a breath slowing, a thought drifting away. Something just feels lighter.

Because the journey of healing is already happening. In fact, it may have already begun.

And perhaps, even now, you can sense something within you

shifting.

Dancing Buddha's Quote

"Healing begins not with a destination, but with a single step inward. The journey is yours to take."

PART ONE

The Self

PART ONE

THE SELF – KNOWING AND NURTURING THE INNER WORLD

The journey of self-awareness is both ancient and ever-renewing, like a mountain standing through the ages while the seasons reshape its face. And perhaps, as you read these words, you may begin to sense that your own journey has already begun—quietly, steadily, like the first breath of morning air.

Self-awareness is the foundation of all meaningful transformation. Without it, love, understanding, and healing remain distant concepts, like stars glimpsed through a cloudy sky. But when we turn inward—when we clear the lens through which we see ourselves—everything becomes brighter, more connected, and easier to navigate.

The monk, with his quiet wisdom, understands this well. His first lessons often turn inward, guiding his students to look into the mirror of their own minds, their own hearts, their own habits.

He does not provide easy answers. Instead, he offers a path. A question. A moment of silence that invites discovery.

In **The Quiet World**, a student seeking wisdom finds it not in spoken teachings, but in the spaces between sound—the hush of wind through the trees, the stillness of a pond, the pause between birdsong. And as he listens, he realizes something... Silence is not empty. It is full of meaning, if only we learn to hear it.

And perhaps, even now, you are beginning to notice... that there is a quiet wisdom within you, waiting to be heard.

Why Begin with the Self?

The self is where everything begins. How we see the world is shaped by the lens of our thoughts, emotions, and past experiences. If that lens is clouded by regret, pain, or misunderstanding, the world appears distorted, confusing, and heavy.

But when that lens is clear... when we see ourselves with honesty and compassion... suddenly, everything shifts. The burdens grow lighter. The world seems softer, more open. And without effort, we begin to move through life with greater ease.

Yet self-awareness is not about fixing something broken. The monk teaches that beneath layers of distraction, fear, and self-judgment, there is something that has always been whole. A quiet, steady light, like the moon behind passing clouds.

But before we can see that light clearly, we must first loosen the knots that bind us.

In **The Golden Cord**, a student struggles with an invisible weight—the past. The monk does not tell him to forget. Instead, he hands the student a tangled cord and asks him to untie it, knot by knot. And as the student works, he begins to understand—healing is not about cutting away what once was. It is about unraveling its hold on us, gently and with patience.

And as you read these words, perhaps a part of you is already sensing... that some knots within you are ready to be loosened.

The Dance of Emotions and Habits

Sometimes, we move through life as if walking through a dense forest in morning mist. The path ahead is unclear. We follow habits, emotions, reactions—often without question. And yet, the monk reminds us:

"Your emotions are not your enemy. They are messengers. Listen to them, but do not let them steer the ship."

Imagine standing in that mist, pausing for a moment, breathing deeply. As you do, the air begins to clear. The trees become visible. The path reveals itself.

The stories in this section invite you to **pause**, to **breathe**, and to let the mist begin to lift.

In **Feeling the Ground**, a student lost in his thoughts learns to stop and sense what is beneath him—not just the earth, but the deeper foundation of his emotions. He realizes that feelings do not simply appear. They have origins—shaped by experience, reaction, and habit.

And as you reflect on this, you might begin to wonder... What emotions have been shaping your path? What habits have guided your steps? And what would happen if, just for a moment, you stood still and listened?

Letting Go of Guilt and Regret

Regret can feel like a heavy stone in a traveler's pack, slowing each step, making even small hills feel like mountains.

And perhaps, there have been times when you have carried this weight, believing it was yours to bear. Many do.

But what if regret was never meant to be a punishment?

What if it was always just a messenger—bringing you wisdom, showing you something you were meant to learn?

In **The Silent Room**, a student struggles to quiet his mind, disturbed by the endless noise of his thoughts. The monk reminds him that the room itself is silent—it is only the sounds within it that shift and change.

And just as the student realizes he is not the noise but the space beneath it, you too may begin to sense...

That you are not your fleeting thoughts.

Not your regrets.

Not the weight you have carried.

Beneath them, you are vast. Open. Still.

And when the lesson is understood, the weight can be set down.

Grounding in the Present Moment

The monk often asks his students to stop and notice the earth beneath their feet.

"The present moment is like the ground," he says. *"It is always here to support you, no matter where you are."*

Yet, so often, the mind wanders—drifting into the past,

reaching toward the future. Thoughts come and go, pulling attention elsewhere. And in that movement, presence is lost—not because it is far away, but because we have stepped out of alignment with it.

But presence is not something to chase. It is something to allow.

Right now, as you read these words, pause for a moment. Notice the spaces between them. Feel the breath moving in and out of your body. Observe the quiet that surrounds you. The mind does not need to be silenced; it only needs to be witnessed.

Stillness is not empty. Silence is not a void. The present moment is alive, full, waiting to be felt.

And perhaps, as you allow yourself to settle into this awareness, you will begin to sense something...

Right now, there is nothing to fix.
Nowhere else to be.
Only this moment, exactly as it is.

And as you breathe into it, you may realize...
The present was never lost.
It was simply waiting for you to arrive.

The Moving Nature of Balance

Balance is often misunderstood as stillness.

But the monk reminds us: true balance is movement. It is constant adjustment, the ability to flow with change rather than resist it.

In **The Pattern of Stones**, students take turns throwing stones onto the ground, watching as patterns form and shift. They observe how the center changes depending on the arrangement of the outer stones.

"Where is the true center?" the monk asks.

The students realize—balance is not a fixed point. It is something that moves.

And as you reflect on this, perhaps you too are beginning to sense... that balance is not something to hold onto. It is something to trust.

An Invitation to Begin

And now, as you reach this moment, you might begin to notice... a quiet opening within you.

A space for curiosity. A gentle unfolding.

This part of the journey is not about forcing change. It is about coming home.

And as you breathe, as you pause, as you feel the quiet space within, you might begin to wonder...

What happens when we let go of the noise? What happens when we listen to the part of ourselves that has always been whole?

The stories ahead will guide you. The meditations will support you. And with each step inward, you may discover...

That you are exactly where you need to be.

Dancing Buddha Quote

"Within you, there has always been a light... steady, untouched by time. And as you consider these words, you may begin to sense... that all we ever do is clear the dust, polish the glass, and allow the light to shine as it was always meant to."

STORY 1 - THE DANCING BUDDHA

The air was heavy with the promise of rain, the kind that stirs the earth and leaves the soul longing for release. A deep hush settled over the monastery grounds, disturbed only by the occasional whisper of wind through the trees. A group of monks gathered beneath the sprawling branches of a bodhi tree, their saffron robes fluttering in the warm breeze. Some stood in quiet contemplation, while others murmured softly, their voices laced with longing.

Among them stood the Buddha, serene and radiant, his eyes reflecting both the clouds above and the hope within each heart before him.

The monks had come seeking answers. Life's burdens weighed heavily upon them—the sorrows of the past, the uncertainties of the future, and the unrelenting pursuit of peace.

They meditated. They practiced detachment. They followed the path of mindfulness. And yet, joy remained elusive.

One monk stepped forward, bowing low before the Buddha. "Master," he said, his voice strained with frustration, "we have followed your teachings, yet joy eludes us. The world is full of suffering, and though we meditate and walk the path, our hearts remain heavy. How can we find joy when the rain of sorrow pours endlessly upon us?"

The Buddha listened in silence, his gaze soft and compassionate. Then, as the first drops of rain began to fall, he smiled.

"Come," he said, rising to his feet and gesturing to the open field beyond the tree. "Let us walk in the rain."

Dancing in the Rain

The monks hesitated; their brows furrowed in confusion. The rain fell harder now, its rhythm steady and insistent, soaking the ground and the hem of their robes. Some instinctively pulled their robes tighter, shielding themselves from the wetness, while others glanced at each other, uncertain of their teacher's intent.

Still, the Buddha stepped forward, his arms outstretched as if embracing the sky.

At first, the monks followed tentatively, their movements stiff and hesitant. The rain clung to their skin, cold and relentless, a reminder of the sorrows they carried. Their feet sank slightly into the softened earth, their sandals collecting specks of mud.

But the Buddha did not simply walk.

He danced.

His feet moved lightly across the wet earth, his laughter ringing out like a bell. He twirled, leapt, and turned, his movements effortless and full of life. He spun beneath the falling drops, his joy as boundless as the storm itself.

The monks stood frozen, watching in stunned silence. The Buddha—revered teacher, master of wisdom—was dancing in the storm like a child.

"Master!" another monk called out, his voice rising above the sound of the rain. "Why do you dance? The rain is cold and uncomfortable. Should we not seek shelter from it?"

The Buddha paused mid-step, his face uplifted to the sky. "The rain does not choose who it falls upon," he said. "It touches all—joyful or sorrowful, wise or foolish. To resist it is to resist life itself. But to dance in the rain is to embrace it, to let it wash away the burdens we cling to so tightly."

He extended his hand to the monk, who hesitated before taking it. Together, they began to dance, slowly at first, then with growing freedom. The monk's steps were awkward, his body resisting the unfamiliarity of surrender. But soon, something within him softened. He let go.

One by one, the other monks watched their teacher, their solemn faces flickering with recognition. The rain was no longer an inconvenience - it was something to be felt, something to be welcomed. Slowly, they too began to move, hesitantly at first, then with growing abandon. Laughter rose like the wind, and soon, all were dancing, their voices ringing out like birds greeting the dawn.

The storm raged on, but in their hearts, the weight had lifted.

Guided Meditation: Letting the Rain Wash You Clean

As the story unfolds, imagine yourself among the monks, standing beneath the bodhi tree. The rain begins to fall, cool and gentle at first, then stronger, until it soaks through your clothes and touches your skin.

Close your eyes. Feel the raindrops on your face, each one a tiny messenger of release. Let their coolness awaken you to the present moment.

Take a deep breath in. Feel the weight of your burdens—the sorrows, fears, and doubts you carry.

As you exhale, imagine the rain washing those burdens away. See them sliding off your shoulders, dissolving into the earth beneath your feet.

Now, envision yourself stepping forward into the rain. Your feet move naturally, effortlessly. With each step, you feel lighter, freer.

You begin to dance. Not for anyone else, but for yourself. The rain is no longer something to endure; it is a partner in your joy.

Let your movements flow. Allow yourself to smile, to laugh, to twirl. Feel the joy that comes not from escaping the storm, but from embracing it.

The Lesson of Joy

When the storm passed, the monks gathered once more beneath the bodhi tree, their robes damp but their spirits light. The earth glistened, cleansed by the rain, the scent of wet leaves filling the air.

One monk stepped forward, his face illuminated with newfound understanding. "Master," he said, "I felt the rain as I have never felt it before. It was not a source of suffering, but of freedom. I danced, not to escape my burdens, but to let them go."

The Buddha nodded, his eyes twinkling like the sun breaking through the clouds. "Joy is not something you find," he said. "It is something you create. It is your birthright, waiting for you to claim it—not in the absence of storms, but in their midst."

The monks bowed in gratitude, their hearts lighter, their path clearer. They had come seeking wisdom, but what they had found was something greater—a way of being.

Affirmation

"Joy is my birthright. I embrace life in all its forms, and I choose to dance with it."

Questions for Reflection

1. What storms in your life feel overwhelming, like the rain in the story? How might you reframe them as opportunities for growth or release?
2. When was the last time you allowed yourself to experience pure, unfiltered joy? What barriers might be preventing you from doing so now?
3. If you were to "dance in the rain" of your life, what might that look like? How can you practice embracing challenges instead of resisting them?

Dancing Buddha's Quote

"Dance, not to escape the rain, but to celebrate it."

Closing Thoughts

The Dancing Buddha reminds us that joy is not the absence of hardship but the ability to embrace life as it comes. The rain, like sorrow, is inevitable, but it is also cleansing, transformative. We can resist it, cower beneath it, or try to outrun it—but in doing so, we miss the beauty of the moment.

By choosing to dance, we reclaim our power. We step out of suffering and into presence, where joy is not something distant but something within us, always waiting to be freed.

No storm lasts forever. But even when it rages, we always have a choice.

Will you stand in fear? Or will you dance?

STORY 2- THE GOLDEN CORD

Introduction: The Knot of Life

Deep in the mountains, where mist draped the treetops and the air hummed with an ancient stillness, a young student sat cross-legged before his master, a venerable monk. The monastery was a haven for seekers, where questions of life, the self, and existence were untangled like the threads of an old tapestry. Today, however, the lesson promised something different.

The monk, his robes flowing like liquid amber, produced a golden cord from his satchel. It gleamed in the sunlight streaming through the temple windows, smooth and radiant, as though it had captured the essence of light itself.

"Do you see this cord?" the monk began, holding it up for the student to see. "It is supple, flexible. It bends, twists, and flows easily in every direction, like water finding its path."

The student nodded, mesmerized by the way the cord danced in the monk's hands.

"This cord is like you when you first arrived here in birth," the monk continued, his voice a soft melody. "Young, open, and curious. You moved through the world with ease, adapting to whatever life presented."

The Weight of Knots

The monk then began tying the cord into knots. Slowly, deliberately, he looped and twisted it, forming one knot after another. The once-fluid motion became halting and rigid. The cord, now tangled, lost its graceful elegance, and the knots crowded together, forming a dense, impenetrable mass.

"Now look," the monk said, holding up the knotted cord. "See how it no longer flows? It is burdened, constrained by its own knots. It is no longer free."

The student frowned. "Why would the cord allow itself to be knotted? Why would it choose this state?"

"Ah," said the monk, smiling, "this is the question. These knots are like the inflexibilities you have built in your own thinking, your own life. They are born each time you feel discomfort with the energy of another and react by closing yourself off."

The student's brow furrowed. "But isn't it natural to protect oneself? To retreat when something feels wrong or overwhelming?"

"Indeed," the monk agreed, "it is natural. But observe the consequences. When you tie a knot to escape discomfort, you may feel temporary relief. Yet over time, these knots accumulate. Your world becomes smaller, more rigid, more painful."

Recognizing the Knots

The student reached for the cord, running his fingers over the tight, unyielding knots. "It does seem crowded now," he murmured. "And painful, too. But how do I know when I am tying these knots?"

"Pain is your signal," the monk said. "When life feels crowded, heavy, or confined, it is a sign that you are clinging to old patterns, old methods that no longer serve you. These knots are your resistance to change, your refusal to adapt when the winds shift."

The student sat silently, reflecting. "So, what must I do? How do I untie the knots?"

The monk smiled again, a twinkle of mischief in his eyes. "You must begin by reexamining your choices. Each knot was tied by you, in moments when you thought you were protecting yourself. Now, you must look at those moments anew."

The Act of Unraveling

He handed the golden cord to the student. "Start with the first knot. Trace it back to its origin. What was the situation? What were you feeling? What belief did you adopt in that moment?"

The student took a deep breath and began to work on the first knot. His fingers moved slowly, methodically, as he retraced the knot's loops and twists. "I remember," he said after a long pause. "I was young, and someone's words stung me. I told myself I would never let anyone hurt me like that again."

"And so, you tied the knot of avoidance," the monk said. "You decided to close yourself off rather than face the discomfort of vulnerability. But what happens when you carry that knot into every interaction?"

The student nodded, his eyes widening with understanding. "I see now. It limits me. It keeps me from connecting, from trusting."

One by one, the student untied the knots, each unraveling a choice made out of fear, defensiveness, or past pain. As he did so, the monk added softly:

"Notice how with every knot you release, the cord becomes lighter and flows more freely. Feel the relief in your heart as you let go."

With each knot undone, the student repeated:

Affirmation 1: *"I am free to release the past and choose peace in the present."*

The monk's voice rose with gentle encouragement, "Yes, with each knot untied, you are choosing a new way. You are embracing change, flexibility, and the freedom to grow."

Guided Meditation: The Golden Cord

The monk gestured for the student to close his eyes. "Let us meditate together to deepen this lesson," he said, his voice steady and calming.

"Breathe deeply," he began, "and imagine yourself holding a golden cord in your hands. Its warmth spreads through your palms, and its glow fills your heart. Perhaps you notice the knots—some small, others large. And as you become aware of them, you might find yourself curious... curious about how easily they might release."

The student inhaled deeply, picturing the cord.

"Now," the monk continued, "choose one knot to untie. As you gently work on it, see a memory surface—a moment from your past. Observe it with compassion, as though you are watching yourself as a child. You see yourself trying to protect, to guard, but now you understand there is no need to hold that tension anymore."

As the knot loosened in his mind, the student whispered:

Affirmation 2: *"I trust in my ability to adapt and flow with life's energies."*

"Feel the freedom as the knot releases," the monk said. "See how the cord becomes smoother, brighter, and more fluid. With each breath, you untie another knot, until the cord flows freely in your hands. It is no longer burdened but radiant and flexible."

The student opened his eyes, his heart light and steady.

Transformation and Freedom

As he worked, the monk spoke. "When you were young, you were innocent, untouched by the burdens of the world. But innocence alone is not enough. True freedom comes through transformation—from understanding your knots and choosing a new way to weave your life."

The student paused, the last knot now undone. The golden cord lay in his lap, shining as it had before, free of its burdens. He looked up at the monk, tears glistening in his eyes. "I feel...free," he said softly.

The monk nodded. "Freedom is not the absence of challenges, but the ability to face them with openness, without tying yourself into knots. Each moment offers a choice: to resist and knot yourself, or to adapt and remain free. You are no longer bound by your past."

The student, with new light in his eyes, placed his hand over his heart and whispered:

Affirmation 3: *"With each knot I release, I discover more of my true self."*

The monk smiled, his heart warm with pride. "You have untied the knots. Now, you will see the world with the clarity of a cord unburdened—able to move in every direction, free and flexible, as you were in the beginning."

As the sun dipped below the horizon, casting the temple in hues of gold and crimson, the monk and student sat in silence, the golden cord glimmering between them—a symbol of freedom, transformation, and the boundless potential within every soul.

Questions for Further Discussion

1. What are some of the "knots" you feel you've tied in your life, and what circumstances or beliefs might have led to them?
2. How can pain or discomfort serve as a signal to recognize the areas where change or release is needed?
3. What steps can you take to begin untying one specific knot in your life? How might this process affect your relationships or personal growth?
4. Reflect on a moment when you chose to adapt instead of resist. How did that decision change your experience?
5. How does the metaphor of the golden cord resonate with your current approach to challenges and growth?

Dancing Buddha's Quote

"True freedom is not the absence of life's challenges but the ability to untie its knots, one breath, one choice at a time."

STORY 3 - THE QUIET WORLD

Introduction

At the edge of a dense forest in Northern India, where ancient cedar trees stood tall and streams whispered through moss-covered stones, a small monastery rested in quiet harmony with the land. The air was cool, carrying the scent of pine needles and fresh earth. The soft hum of insects, the occasional rustle of leaves, and the distant call of a cuckoo bird wove together a symphony of stillness.

Master Ravi, a monk known for his wisdom and warmth, sat beneath a towering banyan tree at the monastery's heart. His orange and maroon robes caught flecks of sunlight that filtered through the tree's branches, and his presence exuded a calm that seemed to draw the world closer.

Gathered before him were six students: Arun, a young man

restless with ambition; Priya, a woman whose grief lingered like a shadow; Sanjay, a farmer weighed down by worry for his crops; and three others, their faces marked with the quiet desperation of inner conflict. They had come seeking peace, though none yet knew how to find it.

Master Ravi let the silence stretch before he spoke, his voice like the first note of a song. "Do you hear that?" he asked.

The students exchanged puzzled looks. "Hear what?" Arun finally asked.

"The world," Ravi said, his eyes soft. "Beneath the birds, beneath the wind. Do you hear its quiet?"

Section 1: The Noise Within

Ravi's gaze rested on Priya. "What noise fills your mind?" he asked gently.

Her voice was barely above a whisper. "It's my sister. I hear her laugh, her voice… but it's gone. And the silence she left behind feels louder than anything."

Ravi nodded, his expression kind. "And you, Arun?"

Arun frowned, shifting on his cushion. "My thoughts don't stop. It's like a drumbeat—plans, goals, things I need to do. It's exhausting."

Sanjay sighed. "For me, it's the weather. The rain, the sun, the clouds. Everything feels like a question I need to answer. It's never quiet."

Ravi leaned forward slightly, his voice steady. "And yet," he said, "if you listen carefully, you might begin to notice something surprising: the noise you hear is not coming from the world around you. It is coming from within."

The students stared at him, confused.

"What you call noise," Ravi continued, "is created by your

mind. The world itself is quiet. Even a storm has silence beneath it. But our noise does not stay within us. We bring it into the world, and it takes form. Wars begin not on battlefields but in minds. Greed, fear, anger—these are storms we create inside, and they ripple outward, disturbing the quiet world around us."

Priya's hands tightened in her lap. "But Master," she said softly, "the memories feel so real. How do I stop them from becoming my whole world?"

Ravi's voice grew gentler. "By noticing that they are not the whole world. The world is wider than your thoughts, Priya. And it is quieter, too."

Section 2: A Lesson in the Country

Ravi rose and gestured for the group to follow him. They left the monastery, walking along a dirt path that wound through fields and meadows. The air was alive with the scent of wildflowers and the earthy smell of damp soil. Bees buzzed lazily from bloom to bloom, their hum blending with the rustle of grass in the breeze.

The group came to a hill overlooking a wide valley. Below them, a river meandered through the land, its surface glinting in the sunlight. Ravi sat on the grass and motioned for the students to do the same.

"Close your eyes," he said. "Take a deep breath. Feel the coolness of the air as it enters your lungs, the warmth as it leaves. Now listen. What do you hear?"

The students began to name the sounds: the chirp of crickets, the murmur of the river, the faint rustle of leaves.

"And beneath that?" Ravi asked.

The group fell silent, their brows furrowing. Priya whispered, "Nothing. It's... quiet."

"Exactly," Ravi said, his voice soft but certain. "The quiet was always there, beneath the noise. Imagine now that your thoughts are like a storm—a loud wind rushing through your mind. Can you feel it?"

The students nodded, their faces tense.

"Now," Ravi said, "imagine the storm has passed. The wind slows, the sky clears. What remains?"

Arun exhaled deeply. "The quiet," he murmured.

"Good," Ravi said. "This is the true nature of the world. But think about this: what happens when we carry our inner storms into the world?" He gestured to the valley below, where they could see a factory by the riverbank, its machines roaring and smoke rising into the air. The water nearby was murky and lifeless.

"This," Ravi said, "is what happens when inner noise takes form. A thought of greed, fear, or anger can ripple outward, creating systems that disturb the harmony of the quiet world. But remember: just as a storm fades, so too can peace begin—with a single calm mind."

Section 3: A Guided Meditation

That evening, Ravi led the students to the meditation hall. Candles cast a golden glow on the stone walls, and the faint scent of sandalwood filled the air. The floor was lined with soft cushions in shades of deep red and gold.

"Sit comfortably," Ravi said, his voice like the low hum of a distant drum. "Close your eyes, and as you take a deep breath, notice how the air feels cool as it enters and warm as it leaves. Let your shoulders drop, your hands rest gently, and your body soften."

The students settled into their breath, their faces relaxing.

"Now," Ravi continued, "imagine a sound in your mind—a thought, a memory, a worry. Hear it clearly. Notice how it feels, as though it is a storm moving through."

Priya's brow furrowed slightly, her hands clenching.

"Now," Ravi said, his voice soothing, "imagine turning the volume down, like a distant echo fading. With each breath, the sound grows softer, quieter, until it is gone. What remains?"

Jia, one of the quieter students, whispered, "Stillness."

"Good," Ravi said. "Now feel how this stillness expands, filling your chest, your mind, and the space around you. Each breath brings you deeper into this quiet. And as you sit here, you may begin to realize that this quiet has always been here, waiting for you to return to it. When your mind is calm, you bring calm to the world."

Section 4: The Sound of Peace

After the meditation, Ravi led the students to a nearby lake. The water was so still it mirrored the stars beginning to emerge in the twilight sky. The scent of blooming jasmine mingled with the earthy aroma of the lake's edge.

"Do you see how calm the water is?" Ravi asked.

The students nodded.

"When the wind blows, the surface ripples," he said. "But the water beneath remains still. Your mind is the same. Thoughts may ripple across it, but beneath them, there is always calm. This is the quiet world. But remember: the ripples of your thoughts can reach far. A single storm in your mind can stir conflict across the waters of the world. And so can your stillness bring peace."

Conclusion

The students left the monastery transformed. Priya felt the storm of her grief subside, replaced by the quiet love of her sister's memory. Arun realized he didn't have to chase his ambitions to find peace—they could unfold naturally. Sanjay discovered that no matter the weather, the quiet world within him remained untouched.

Master Ravi stood by the lake, watching the ripples fade into stillness as the students walked away. The world around him hummed with life—the whisper of the wind, the distant call of a bird, the faint rustle of leaves. And yet, beneath it all, there was silence. He smiled, knowing his students had begun to hear it, too.

Affirmations

"I can return to the quiet world within me, where peace always resides."

"Beneath every thought, there is a calm that cannot be disturbed."

Questions for Further Discussion

1. How does the noise in your mind affect your perception of the world?
2. In what ways can your inner peace influence the world around you?
3. How can you remind yourself to return to the quiet world during moments of stress?
4. What external systems or conflicts do you notice that might stem from inner noise?

5. How can we collectively create more ripples of peace in the world?

Dancing Buddha's Quote

"The storms of the mind shape the noise of the world. To quiet the world, calm the mind, and let peace ripple outward."

Gregory K. Cadotte

STORY 4 – FEELING THE GROUND

Introduction

The monastery sat perched on the hillside like a guardian over the valley below. As the sun dipped low, the hills were bathed in amber light, and the wind carried the faint scent of jasmine and pine. It was a time of peace for most, but for Ravi, the quiet surroundings only deepened his inner turmoil.

Inside the stone meditation hall, shadows lengthened as the evening light filtered through narrow windows. Ravi paced back and forth across the polished wooden floor. His thoughts churned like storm clouds, each step echoing his frustration.

Earlier that day, during the temple's sacred evening recitation, Arun had corrected Ravi's mispronunciation of a verse. The correction had been sharp, made publicly in front of the entire assembly. It had stung—not just his pride but something deeper.

He had worked tirelessly to master the chants, and Arun's words felt like a dismissal of all his effort.

"Why would he do that?" Ravi muttered, clenching his fists. "Does he think he's better than me? He had no right to humiliate me like that!"

He stopped pacing as the soft creak of the hall's door announced the arrival of Master Dev, the monastery's head monk. Clad in simple robes, Master Dev's presence filled the room like a steadying breeze, his calm demeanor contrasting sharply with Ravi's agitation.

"Ravi," the monk said, his voice low and grounding, "what troubles your heart so deeply that you've come to battle the silence of this hall?"

Ravi hesitated, caught between his anger and his respect for the teacher. Finally, the words spilled out. "Arun embarrassed me today during the ceremony. He corrected me in front of everyone! I can't stop thinking about it. I feel so... angry!"

Master Dev regarded Ravi with steady eyes, his expression neither condemning nor indulgent. "Come," he said gently, motioning to a spot on the floor. "Sit with me. Let us see what your anger has to say."

The Lesson Begins

The monk settled cross-legged on the floor, his movements deliberate, like flowing water. Ravi sat across from him, his body tense.

Without speaking, Master Dev extended his leg and tapped his foot lightly on the ground. The soft sound echoed in the stillness.

"Ravi," he asked, his tone thoughtful, "what am I feeling?"

Ravi blinked, confused by the question. "The ground,

Master," he replied after a moment.

"No," Master Dev said, shaking his head gently. "I have never felt the ground. I am feeling my foot. The ground itself feels nothing; it is neutral, unchanging. The sensation is in me, not in the earth. Do you understand?"

Ravi frowned, unsure. "I think so, but what does that have to do with my anger?"

The monk leaned forward slightly, his gaze intent. "Your anger feels as though it is about Arun's words. But where do you truly feel this anger? Is it in his words? Is it in him?"

Ravi hesitated, then placed a hand over his chest. "It's... here. Inside me."

"Exactly," Master Dev said, his voice soft yet firm. "Your anger is not in Arun's actions or his correction. It lives within you, as your foot feels the ground. The words themselves are like the earth—still and unfeeling. Your reaction gives them power. Do you see?"

Exploring the Storm

Ravi's brow furrowed as he grappled with the monk's words. "So... you're saying my anger isn't his fault? That it's all... me?"

"This is not about fault, Ravi," Master Dev replied gently. "Your anger is neither good nor bad—it simply exists. But it is born of your perception, the story you've told yourself about what happened. If you change the story, the feeling changes too."

Ravi's shoulders sagged slightly as the tension began to drain. "I... don't know if I can just change how I feel."

Master Dev smiled, his expression one of infinite patience. "You cannot force feelings to change, but you can observe them. Close your eyes, Ravi. Sit with your anger as you would sit with an old friend. What does it feel like? Where does it sit in your body? Is it heavy or light? Still or moving?"

Ravi closed his eyes and took a deep breath. He felt the fiery heat in his chest, the tightness in his shoulders, the restless energy coursing through him. Slowly, as he named each sensation, the anger began to lose its sharp edges.

"It's changing," he said softly. "It doesn't feel so overwhelming anymore."

Master Dev nodded. "That is the nature of emotions. They rise and fall like waves. When you observe them without judgment, you see them for what they are: temporary. Now, ask yourself this, Ravi—what if, instead of anger, you chose curiosity? Why might Arun have corrected you? What was his intention?"

Ravi opened his eyes, the monk's question lingering in his mind. "I… I don't know. Maybe he wasn't trying to embarrass me. Maybe he just wanted me to get it right."

Guided Meditation: Feeling the Ground

Master Dev rose and gestured for Ravi to follow him. Together, they stepped out into the courtyard. The moon hung low, casting the garden in soft silver light. The cool night air carried the faint scent of pine.

"Remove your sandals," Master Dev instructed. "Feel the earth beneath your feet."

Ravi obeyed, the cool stone grounding him.

"Close your eyes," the monk continued. "Feel the texture of the stone—the coolness, its solidity. Imagine roots growing from the soles of your feet, anchoring you to the earth. With every breath, let the tension in your body flow downward, into the soil, where it can dissolve. And as you breathe in, imagine calm and strength rising through those roots."

Ravi stood in silence, the vivid imagery guiding his awareness inward. The cool ground felt steady, unchanging. The anger he had carried for hours now seemed like a distant echo.

"Repeat after me," Master Dev said softly.

1. *"I am not my emotions; I am the awareness behind them."*

2. *"I am grounded, calm, and free."*

Ravi whispered the words, their meaning sinking deeply into his heart.

Resolution and Reflection

The next morning, Ravi approached Arun, who was kneeling in the herb garden, carefully pruning the basil plants.

"Arun," Ravi began, his voice steady but tentative. "About yesterday... I wanted to thank you."

Arun looked up, surprised. "Thank me? For what?"

"For correcting me," Ravi said. "I reacted poorly, but I realize now that you weren't trying to embarrass me. You were helping me."

A smile spread across Arun's face. "I'm glad you see it that way. I wasn't trying to upset you—I just wanted to honor the chant."

Master Dev watched from a distance, a faint smile on his lips. He knew that Ravi had taken an important step, but he also knew the path of self-awareness was a lifelong journey.

Questions for Further Discussion

1. How do the stories we tell ourselves influence our emotions?
2. What techniques from the story can you use to observe and transform your emotions?
3. Have you ever misinterpreted someone's actions? How did it feel to gain clarity?
4. How can grounding practices like the meditation described help you in moments of emotional overwhelm?

Dancing Buddha's Quote

"The ground does not tremble under your feet, nor does the sky cry out when the storm passes. Be like the earth—steady, patient, and kind. From stillness comes clarity; from clarity, peace."

STORY 5 – THE BANYAN'S LESSON – BEYOND THE INNER CHILD

Introduction

On the edge of a serene forest, a wise monk named Master Evan lived in a small monastery. His reputation as a teacher of inner peace drew seekers from far and wide. Among them were three students: John, Sarah, and Michael. Each carried a heavy burden.

John was haunted by the shadow of his past failures, a weight he could not seem to put down. Sarah wrestled daily with the fire of unresolved anger, which burned through her joy. Michael, the quietest of the three, struggled with self-doubt, constantly questioning his worth.

Master Evan, known for his transformative wisdom and ability to weave profound truths into simple stories, took them under his care. One day, he gathered the students under a sprawling banyan tree, its ancient roots tangled like the intricate connections between body, mind, and spirit.

The Lesson Begins

Master Evan began, his voice steady and soothing, "There is an illusion many hold—the 'inner child,' a being frozen in time, trapped in emotion. But what if I told you there is no intrinsic inner child? Instead, there is the inner self, bound by the grip of emotional trauma and halted growth leaving you a child within. Today, we will explore this truth."

John furrowed his brow. "But isn't healing about nurturing this inner child? How do we care for it if it's not real?"

Master Evan smiled. "Healing doesn't come from indulging illusions. It comes from understanding and release. Let us walk this path together."

Scene One: John's Doubt

As they walked deeper into the forest, Master Evan gestured to a young sapling bowed low beneath a heavy vine. Its branches strained under the weight.

"Imagine this tree is your inner self," he said. "The vine represents your emotional trauma. The tree bends not because it is weak, but because the vine binds it so. Would you care for the tree by watering the vine?"

John shook his head, a flicker of understanding dawning. "No. I'd remove the vine."

"Exactly," Master Evan said. "To nurture the tree, you release it from what constrains it. Likewise, caring for your inner self means addressing the childish patterns born of trauma, not coddling them. Now ask yourself: what vines have you been watering?"

John touched the tree, closing his eyes. "I've been watering the vine, haven't I?" he murmured.

Master Evan nodded. "Yes, but the moment you decide to release it, you allow your true self to grow. Imagine yourself as the tree—strong, resilient, free."

Scene Two: Sarah's Anger

By midday, they reached a stream, its waters clear and fast-moving. Sarah paused, her frustration rising like a storm cloud. "I don't understand," she said, her voice sharp. "Every time I think of my childhood, I feel anger welling up inside me. How can I not hold on to it?"

Master Evan knelt by the stream, scooping water into his hands. "Look closely," he said. "When I hold this water, it appears still, but it is not. It yearns to flow. Letting go is not an act of weakness—it is freeing what longs to move. Your anger is like this water. It becomes stagnant only when you hold it."

Sarah stared at the water slipping through his fingers. "But what if it comes back?"

Master Evan's tone softened. "Letting go is not a one-time act but a practice. Each time anger rises, let it flow again, until its path becomes so smooth that peace follows naturally. And now, as you look at this stream, you might find yourself feeling calmer, lighter, more at ease."

Sarah dipped her hands into the water, feeling its cool flow. Something shifted within her, subtle but profound. She felt as though a bird's wing had brushed her soul, leaving a faint yet undeniable impression.

Scene Three: Michael's Self-Doubt

Later, as the group rested beneath a towering oak tree, Michael spoke hesitantly. "I always feel like I'm not enough," he admitted, his voice barely audible. "It's as though I'm still the child who failed to meet expectations."

Master Evan nodded and gestured for Michael to close his eyes. "Let us journey inward together," he said, his tone becoming softer, almost hypnotic.

Guided Meditation

Master Evan's voice was like a gentle stream, guiding Michael deeper. "Michael, as you close your eyes, notice the steady rhythm of your breath. Feel the warmth of the sun on your skin, the softness of the meadow beneath you. Now, imagine the child before you. See their small hands, their wide eyes, their vulnerability.

"As you kneel before this child, you might notice a shift—a sense of connection or understanding. And as you look into their eyes, you may realize that this child is not separate from you, but part of a whole, present and strong."

Michael's lips trembled. "I see them dissolving," he whispered.

"Yes," Master Evan continued. "And as they dissolve, what remains is your true self—whole, resilient, enough. With every breath, you feel this truth anchoring within you."

The Lesson Unfolds

When Michael opened his eyes, he felt lighter, as though a burden he had carried for years had been set down.

Master Evan addressed them all, his gaze steady and warm. "The illusion of the inner child is a placeholder for pain. True healing does not come from treating the self as a wounded child but as a whole being capable of growth and transformation. It's not about clinging to the past but moving beyond it."

The students listened in silence, each absorbing the lesson in their own way.

Conclusion

Back at the monastery, the students reflected on the day's journey.

John spoke first. "I see now how I've been watering my own vines. It's time to stop."

Sarah nodded, her voice softer than usual. "I think I understand what it means to let go. It's not giving up—it's setting myself free."

Michael, still emotional but steady, added, "I feel... enough, for the first time."

Master Evan smiled. "You've each taken a step toward freedom. Remember: you are not defined by your past. You hold the key to your own liberation. Release what no longer serves you, and you'll discover the strength that was always within."

The students bowed deeply, gratitude shining in their eyes.

Affirmations

"I release the vines of my past and allow my true self to grow—strong, resilient, and free."

"I am whole and capable in this moment; I move forward with clarity, unburdened by illusion."

Questions for Reflection

1. What emotions or memories act as the "vines" that constrain your inner self?
2. How can you practice releasing what no longer serves you?
3. What steps can you take to view yourself as whole and capable in the present moment?
4. How does letting go create space for growth in your life?

Dancing Buddha's Quote

"The self held as a child by pain remains stagnant. The self embraced by understanding moves forward, free from illusion."

STORY 6 - THE STILLNESS WITHIN: A PATH TO FREEDOM

Introduction

In the quiet serenity of a mountain monastery, the winds whispered through the trees, the stone walls stood firm and silent, and the sunlight filtered through the leaves in soft, golden beams. There, in the peaceful calm of the temple courtyard, a monk and his student sat in contemplation. The student, eager but restless, had been studying under the monk's tutelage for many months, learning the ways of meditation, patience, and inner stillness. Yet, in his heart, a storm of questions churned, and he found himself unable to grasp the deeper truths his master spoke of.

The Test of Stillness

On that particular afternoon, the monk asked the student to stand and prepare for a lesson.

"Today," said the monk, his voice calm but firm, "we will test your stillness. You must remain grounded, no matter the challenge."

The student nodded, his brow furrowing in both anticipation and doubt. He had learned much from the monk—how to sit in silence, how to watch his thoughts without attachment—but still, he struggled with the sensations of discomfort that arose during his practice. His body was young and strong, yet his mind was often troubled by the smallest distraction. He had not yet fully learned to control his reaction to the world.

"Stand in front of me," the monk instructed.

The student stood tall, breathing deeply, trying to settle his thoughts.

Without warning, the monk raised his hand and swung it toward the student's face in a swift motion. It was as if the monk was about to strike, but just before contact, he stopped—his hand hovering inches from the student's skin.

The student flinched, his whole body tensing as he instinctively took a step back.

The Nature of Reaction

"Why do you move?" the monk asked, his voice soft but steady, his eyes searching.

The student, his breath shallow and fast, took a moment to

regain his composure. His heart beat loudly in his chest as he slowly exhaled, trying to find his voice.

"Master, I... I thought you were going to strike me," he said, his voice betraying both confusion and a touch of fear.

The monk nodded, lowering his hand. "Yes, you thought I was going to strike you. And because you thought this, you reacted. You flinched. You stepped away. But you did not wait to see whether the strike would actually come. You reacted as though it were already a reality."

Pain of Body and Mind

"You believe the strike would have caused you harm, don't you?" the monk continued, his voice full of understanding, yet unwavering. "That it would have caused you physical pain, injury, discomfort."

The student nodded. "Yes, Master. Of course, I would have been hurt."

The monk stepped back and observed him with a steady gaze. "But tell me," he said after a pause, "what kind of pain would have been worse for you—pain of the body, or pain of the mind and heart?"

The student hesitated. He had always understood pain as something physical, something that could be healed or avoided. But the monk's question made him think of a deeper pain, one that was less visible but perhaps just as dangerous.

Understanding the Connection

"Master," the student asked, his voice trembling slightly, "what do you mean by that?"

The monk gestured for the student to sit, and they both settled onto the cool stone floor of the courtyard. "Let me explain," the monk said. "You feared that I might strike you because you imagined the physical pain it would cause. But in doing so, you forgot something important. Pain, both physical and emotional, is connected. When you experience physical injury, the body suffers, but the mind also reacts to that suffering. Your thoughts become clouded with the pain, your emotions become tangled with fear, frustration, or anger."

The student's brow furrowed. "But what does that have to do with emotions?"

The monk smiled gently. "When you face emotional pain—whether it be sadness, anger, or fear—it is no different. The pain of the heart and mind causes suffering in the same way. But we often do not see this connection. We separate the two kinds of pain—body and mind—as though they are independent. We think of emotional suffering as something that can be ignored or overcome, while we treat physical pain with care and attention. But in truth, both are the same. They both arise from a disturbance within, and both can cloud our perception, limiting our ability to live freely."

Observing Without Reaction

The student listened intently, still unsure but sensing that the monk was leading him to something profound.

"When you are struck," the monk continued, "and when the body is injured, your movements become slower, more cautious. You are less mobile, less flexible. Your focus shifts entirely to the wound, and your mind becomes preoccupied with the pain. The same happens when you are emotionally injured. Your thoughts become entangled in fear, sorrow, or regret. You become less patient with yourself, less able to move freely in your life."

The student nodded slowly, beginning to grasp the wisdom in the monk's words.

A Guided Meditation

The monk stood and gestured for the student to follow him to a shaded grove nearby. The sunlight filtered through the leaves, creating a dappled pattern on the soft grass. The sound of a gentle stream nearby added a calming rhythm to the scene.

"Sit here," the monk instructed, pointing to a flat stone near the stream. "Close your eyes and listen to my voice."

The student obeyed, folding his legs and resting his hands on his knees. The monk's voice softened, becoming a soothing guide.

"Begin by taking a deep breath. Inhale through your nose… and exhale slowly through your mouth. Feel the air entering your body, filling your chest and your belly. And as you exhale, let go of any tension you may be holding."

The student's breathing slowed, matching the rhythm of the monk's words.

"Now, imagine you are a tree," the monk continued. "Your roots sink deep into the earth, drawing strength and stability from the soil. Feel your connection to the ground beneath you, solid and unwavering."

The student's shoulders relaxed as he visualized the roots anchoring him.

"Above, your branches stretch toward the sky, reaching for the light. Each leaf is open, absorbing the warmth of the sun. Feel the energy flowing through you, from the earth to the sky, grounding you and lifting you at the same time."

The monk's voice grew softer. "Now, notice the stream

nearby. Its waters flow effortlessly, moving around stones and roots without resistance. Picture your thoughts as leaves on the surface of the water. Watch them drift by, carried away by the current. There is no need to hold onto them; simply let them pass."

A sense of calm enveloped the student as he visualized the flowing stream.

"Take a moment to rest in this stillness. You are the tree, steady and strong. You are the stream, flowing and free. Whatever arises, you can observe it without attachment. Breathe in this peace and carry it with you."

The monk fell silent, allowing the sound of the stream to fill the space. Minutes passed before he spoke again.

"When you are ready, open your eyes."

The student opened his eyes slowly, the world around him seeming brighter and more vivid. A deep sense of tranquility filled his heart.

The monk smiled gently. "This stillness you have found is the foundation of true freedom," he said. "Carry it with you as we continue."

The Path to Freedom

The student sat in silence, absorbing the lesson. The monk watched him for a moment before continuing.

"You see," the monk said gently, "freedom is not the absence of pain, but the ability to face it without becoming bound by it. Pain—whether of the body or the heart—only holds power over us when we resist it or react blindly. But if you can observe it with patience, without attachment or fear, then you will begin to loosen its grip."

The student took a deep breath, feeling the weight of the

monk's words settle within him.

The monk's voice softened further. "When suffering arises, do not fight it. Do not battle your emotions when they come—whether pain, anger, or fear. Instead, ask yourself: What is their cause? What belief or thought is keeping me bound to them? If you react with anger, you feed the anger. If you react with fear, you deepen the fear. But if you remain still, if you look inward with an open heart, you will see that the cause of your suffering can be understood—and transformed."

A gentle breeze moved through the grove, rustling the leaves above them. The student closed his eyes, letting the words settle within him like ripples on a still pond.

"True freedom," the monk continued, "lies not in escaping pain, but in transcending it. When you no longer see pain as an enemy, you begin to recognize it as a teacher. All suffering is a call to awareness. And in that awareness, healing begins."

The student nodded, his heart steady. The monk gave a final instruction:

"Say to yourself: I am not my pain, but the observer of it. I choose to see the causes of my suffering with clarity, and I release them with compassion."

The student repeated the words silently, feeling their truth resonate within him.

Affirmations

"I am not my pain, but the observer of it."

"I choose to see the causes of my suffering with clarity, and I release them with compassion."

Questions for Further Discussion

1. How can you distinguish between reacting to pain and observing it?
2. In what ways can you tend to emotional wounds with the same care as physical ones?
3. What triggers in your life cause suffering, and how might you address their root causes?
4. How does recognizing the connection between body and mind shift your perspective on pain and healing?

Dancing Buddha's Quote

"The path to peace is not in avoiding life's storms but in learning to find stillness
within them."

STORY 7 - THE NATURE OF BALANCE

Introduction

In the tranquil embrace of the mountains, nestled in a secluded valley where time seemed to slow, there lived a wise monk named Renzu. Known for his profound teachings on balance, Renzu guided many through life's complexities. Among his students were Aiko and Kiyoshi, two eager souls seeking wisdom. Aiko, with her quick mind, and Kiyoshi, with his introspective heart, were as different as day and night, yet both were drawn to Renzu's teachings.

One quiet afternoon, as the sky painted itself in hues of orange and gold, Renzu gathered his students near the temple. The air carried the scent of pine, mingling with the distant murmur of a flowing stream. Above them, a bluebird soared gracefully, its feathers glistening like sapphires in the sunlight. "Aiko, Kiyoshi," Renzu began, his voice gentle yet firm, "today, I will teach you about balance. Not a balance that is rigid or fixed, but one that flows like the stream and grows with time. Balance is not something you find; it is something you allow to emerge." The students exchanged curious glances. How could balance emerge rather than be achieved?

The Shifting Center of Balance

Renzu led them to a stone garden where the ground was smooth, and the air was still. Beside a large boulder lay a collection of smooth stones of varying sizes.

"Each of you," Renzu instructed, "will pick up stones and throw them into the air with intention. Observe where they land and how the center of the pattern shifts. This center represents balance, but not in the way you might think."

Aiko, eager to begin, selected a handful of stones. She felt their coolness and weight before throwing the first stone high into the air. It spun gracefully before landing a few feet to her right.

Kiyoshi followed, his movements slower and more deliberate. His stone arced and landed slightly to the left.

Renzu pointed to where the stones had fallen. "Do you see? Each stone creates a different pattern. The center of your balance is never fixed—it changes with every throw."

Aiko frowned. "But Master, isn't balance about finding a fixed point where everything aligns?"

Renzu shook his head gently. "Balance is not a fixed point, Aiko. It is a dynamic force, like the currents of a stream. Just as the stream adjusts its flow around rocks in its path, balance shifts as life acts upon us."

Balance and the Broadening of Experience

As the students gazed at the garden, Kiyoshi asked, "Master, how do we know when our balance is true and not just a response to incomplete understanding?"

Renzu's expression softened. "Much of what we feel—fear, anger, resentment—arises from incomplete understanding. We perceive imbalance because we see only part of the whole. True balance arises when we expand our awareness and experiences." He picked up a small stone and a larger one. "When your life is like this small stone," he said, "it feels balanced but fragile, requiring little to tip it over. As you grow through knowledge and experience, you become like this larger stone—broad, steady, and resilient."

Aiko tilted her head. "So, having less experience can feel balanced, but it's shallow?"

"Yes," Renzu replied. "When you limit your experiences, you limit your understanding. The more you experience and learn, the deeper your balance becomes. It grows with you."

He gestured to the bluebird that landed briefly on a branch. "See the bird? It does not fight the air; it trusts it. Balance is not about control—it's about flow, trust, and adapting to the world as it is."

The Stranger's Dilemma

As they reflected on the lesson, a villager approached, his face lined with worry. Bowing deeply, he said, "Master Renzu, please help me. My daughter wishes to leave the village to study in the city, but I fear for her safety. I act out of love, but she calls me overbearing. How can love bring such conflict?"

Renzu picked up a stone from the garden and handed it to the man. "Hold this tightly," he said.

The man clenched his fist around the stone, his knuckles turning white.

"Now, imagine this stone is your love for your daughter," Renzu continued. "When you hold it this way, what do you feel?"

The man furrowed his brow. "It's hard. Unyielding. Heavy in my grasp."

Renzu nodded. Then, he took a nearby bowl of water and placed it in front of the man. "Now, open your hand and place the stone in the water."

The man did as he was told, watching as the stone settled at the bottom. His fingers, now open and relaxed, felt the coolness of the water around them.

"What do you feel now?" Renzu asked.

The man looked at his open palm, then at the stone resting in the water. "The weight is still there," he admitted, "but it no longer burdens my hand. The water holds it for me."

Renzu smiled. "Love is like this. When you cling too tightly, it becomes rigid—burdensome. But when you release control and allow it to flow, love does not disappear. It simply finds a more natural way to exist."

The man stared at the water for a long moment before nodding slowly. "I see now. I must love her not by gripping, but by supporting—like the water holds the stone."

Renzu's eyes gleamed with approval. "Yes. Trust that she will find her way. Love does not weaken when it is given freedom; it deepens."

The man bowed deeply before leaving, a newfound understanding settling in his heart.

Guided Meditation: Balance in the River of Life

That evening, Renzu brought the students to the banks of a stream. The water flowed gently, adapting to the rocks in its path. "Close your eyes," Renzu instructed, his voice steady and rhythmic. "Breathe deeply. Feel the ground beneath you, solid and unwavering. Hear the stream, its flow constant and free."

The students' breathing slowed as they listened to the water.

"Now," Renzu continued, "imagine you are standing by this stream. In your hand, you hold a stone—a stone that carries something you cling to: a fear, an expectation, or a memory. Feel its weight."

Aiko imagined her need to prove herself. Kiyoshi thought of his fear of failure.

"Step closer to the stream," Renzu said. "See how the water flows around the rocks, unbothered. When you are ready, release your stone. Watch it sink and become part of the current. Notice how the stream carries it, leaving you lighter, freer."

The students visualized the release, feeling a sense of peace.

"Repeat after me," Renzu said:

1. *I release my need to control, trusting the flow of life.'*

2. *'I grow more balanced as my awareness expands.'"*

Their voices, soft yet steady, blended with the stream's sound. "Now," Renzu concluded, "imagine the stream widening, flowing into rivers, lakes, and the vast ocean. Let your balance grow with each experience, steady and interconnected."

The Lesson of Stones

The next day, Aiko and Kiyoshi returned to the garden to observe their pattern of stones. They no longer saw randomness but a dynamic map of shifting centers, each unique and interconnected.

"Balance," Aiko said, "isn't about fixing the stones in place. It's about seeing the beauty in how they fall."

Kiyoshi nodded. "And as our experiences grow, so does our ability to hold balance more deeply."

Renzu, watching from the shade, smiled. "Balance is not a destination but a journey. It flows from love, trust, and the willingness to grow."

Conclusion

As the bluebird soared into the open sky, Aiko and Kiyoshi stood in quiet reflection. The pattern of stones was no longer a puzzle but a testament to life's shifting beauty.

"Balance," Renzu said, "is not about control but trust—trust in the flow of life, in the interconnectedness of all things. With each experience, your balance deepens, allowing you to embrace the world with love and resilience."

Questions for Further Discussion

1. What stones do you carry in your life, and how do they affect your balance?
2. How can broadening your experiences lead to a deeper sense of balance?
3. How does trusting life's flow help you navigate challenges?
4. What does it mean to balance trust and awareness in relationships?

Dancing Buddha's Quote

"Balance grows not by avoiding the winds of life but by letting them strengthen your roots. Love expands when you trust the stream to carry your stones."

STORY 8 - THE SILENT ROOM

Introduction

High atop a misty mountain, nestled between ancient pine trees, stood a humble monastery known as the Temple of the Still Mind. Its walls, weathered by time, seemed to breathe with the silence of the ages. Here, Master Oren, a wise and compassionate teacher, guided his students to uncover the relationship between their Wise Adult and Inner Wounded Child.

On a crisp autumn morning, two of his most devoted students, Aiko and Ren, sat cross-legged before him in the meditation hall. The room was simple—bare wooden floors, a single candle flickering at the center, and the scent of sandalwood lingering in the air. Outside, the wind whispered through the trees, carrying with it the first golden leaves of the season.

Aiko carried a hidden burden: memories of rejection and loneliness that had shadowed her since childhood. Ren, though outwardly confident, was plagued by an endless striving for perfection, driven by the voice of an inner critic that never seemed satisfied.

Master Oren began, his voice gentle yet resonant. "Today, I will take you to the Silent Room. It is a place where your Inner Wounded Child and Wise Adult can meet."

The students exchanged curious glances but said nothing. They had learned long ago that Master Oren's teachings unfolded like a lotus—slowly, beautifully, and in their own time.

The Journey

The trio descended a winding path into a hidden valley, where the air grew warmer and the sound of a distant waterfall grew louder. Along the way, a small monkey began to follow them, chattering and leaping between the trees. Ren laughed at its antics, but Aiko frowned.

"It's distracting," she muttered.

Master Oren smiled knowingly. "The monkey is like the voices of our Inner Wounded Child—loud, persistent, and unpredictable. Observe it without judgment. Let it accompany us, for even the noise has a lesson to teach."

As they continued, a sudden storm rolled in, and the sky darkened. Rain began to fall in sharp, cold drops, and the trail grew slick with mud. Ren, who had been amused by the monkey, now grew frustrated as the wet conditions ruined his perfectly folded robes.

"Why must the journey be so difficult?" he grumbled.

Oren paused and gestured to the monkey, now huddled beneath a tree. "Even the monkey has found a way to sit with the storm. Can you?"

Ren sighed but nodded, pulling his cloak tighter and focusing on each careful step.

After an hour's walk, they arrived at a modest wooden hut. "This," said Master Oren, "is the Silent Room."

The students stepped inside. The hut was bare except for a low table and two cushions. The air was utterly still, as if sound itself had forgotten this place. The silence was profound, enveloping them like a thick, invisible blanket.

At the center of the room stood an unlit lantern. Oren motioned toward it. "This lantern represents the light of your Wise Adult. To illuminate it, you must first sit with the darkness."

Observing the Noise

As they settled onto the cushions, the monkey slipped inside and perched on a rafter above them. It began to chatter loudly, breaking the silence.

"Master," Ren said, his brow furrowing, "how can this be the Silent Room with all this noise?"

Oren's eyes twinkled. "The room is silent. The noise has entered, but the silence remains. The monkey's chatter is like the Inner Wounded Child's voice—full of need, longing, and fear. The silence is your Wise Adult—steady, grounded, and compassionate. Watch the noise. Observe it. Do not become it."

The students closed their eyes, following their master's guidance. The monkey's chattering filled the space, but slowly, Aiko and Ren began to notice something remarkable. Beneath the noise, the silence persisted, unshaken and vast.

"This is like the mind," Oren explained. "The noise is your Inner Wounded Child—its fears, memories, and traumas calling for attention. But beneath it lies your Wise Adult—the silent, compassionate observer. Let the Wise Adult hold the child with kindness. Watch without judgment."

The Inner Journey

Ren struggled with thoughts of inadequacy. No matter how much he achieved, a voice within him whispered, You are not enough. He imagined this voice as a small, frightened child pacing back and forth, seeking reassurance.

"Master," he said, "the noise feels so real, so persistent. How can I see it for what it is?"

Oren placed a hand on Ren's shoulder. "Imagine the noise as the monkey. It leaps, chatters, and demands your attention. But you are not the monkey. You are the Wise Adult watching it. Ask this child what it needs. Perhaps it simply needs to be held."

Ren closed his eyes and imagined kneeling before the small, frightened child. He reached out, offering reassurance. The child's pacing slowed, and its voice softened, leaving behind a profound silence.

Aiko, meanwhile, wept softly as she confronted the fears and traumas she had buried for years. She felt like a storm raged within her, tearing at her heart.

Oren knelt beside her. "Aiko, what does the storm need?"

She looked at him through her tears. "I don't know. It just feels so overwhelming."

"Sometimes," Oren said, "the storm needs nothing but your kindness. Imagine your Wise Adult holding your Inner Wounded Child as you would a frightened little one. Sit with it, and it will begin to calm."

As they both continued their inner work, Oren lit the lantern at the center of the room. Its gentle glow filled the space, a reminder of the light that exists even in the darkest moments.

The Unchanging Silence

As the day turned to evening, the students opened their eyes. The room was dark now, lit only by the glow of the lantern and the setting sun through the window. The monkey stirred, stretched, and scampered outside, leaving them in peace.

Master Oren spoke once more. "The Silent Room is not just this hut. It is within you, always. Your Wise Adult holds the space, no matter how loud the noise, how fierce the storm, or how persistent the monkey. Return to it whenever you are lost."

Aiko and Ren bowed deeply, their hearts lighter, their minds quieter.

As they made their way back to the monastery under a sky painted with stars, the students noticed the monkey following them again, chattering softly.

This time, Aiko reached out and gently fed it a piece of fruit. She smiled, realizing the monkey's chatter no longer disturbed her—it had simply become part of the symphony of life.

Guided Meditation: The Silent Room Within

"Close your eyes," Oren said, as the students sat in the meditation hall later that evening.

"Imagine a room within you, vast and still. Its walls are made of light, and its floor stretches endlessly. This is your Silent Room.

Now, imagine your Inner Wounded Child entering the room. See their small, tender form. They are not the noise; they are simply asking for love. Your Wise Adult greets them with warmth, inviting them to sit in the stillness.

Feel how the silence holds both of you, unshaken. With each

breath, the child grows calmer, their voice quieter. The silence expands, vast and eternal. Know that this room is always within you, a sanctuary no noise can disturb."

The students sat for a long time, their breaths steady, their hearts calm.

Affirmations

"I am the Wise Adult, holding my Inner Wounded Child with love and compassion."

"The silence within me is my sanctuary, where healing begins."

Questions for Reflection

What does your Inner Wounded Child need from you in this moment?
How can your Wise Adult create space for silence and healing?
What might change if you welcomed your inner noise with compassion instead of resistance?

Dancing Buddha's Quote

"The storm may rage, the monkey may chatter, yet the silence holds them both. Be the Wise Adult, and you will find peace."

PART TWO
Relationships

Gregory K. Cadotte

PART TWO

RELATIONSHIPS – LOVE, CONNECTION, AND COMPASSION

The Threads of Connection

Take a moment and bring to mind a relationship in your life—one that has shaped you, that has brought joy or even challenge. Notice how it feels in your body as you recall it. Do you sense warmth, or perhaps tension? Just observe without judgment.

Relationships are the threads that weave the fabric of our lives. Whether with family, friends, partners, or even strangers, our connections shape our joys, our sorrows, and the meaning we derive from life. And like a tapestry, these threads can be smooth or frayed, vibrant or dull. Yet, every thread holds significance.

Right now, as you read this, you might find yourself recalling moments of deep connection, times when love flowed effortlessly. And perhaps, you also remember times when love felt conditional, tied to expectations or circumstances. And that's perfectly natural, isn't it? Because love, like breath, expands and contracts.

The Nature of Love: Unconditional and Conditional

Love is one of the most potent forces in existence. But love is not static. It moves, it shifts, it evolves. Some forms of love nourish and uplift, while others burden and exhaust.

Think for a moment about conditional love. It often sounds like, *"I will love you if..."* or *"I will feel loved when..."* These statements turn love into a transaction, where its presence depends on actions, behaviors, or outcomes. And as you consider this, notice if a memory arises—perhaps a time when love felt just out of reach, tethered to an expectation. And that's okay. Just allow that thought to drift like a passing cloud.

Now, shift your awareness to unconditional love. Imagine a vast ocean, its waves flowing freely, nourishing everything in its path. This is love that simply is—without needing to be earned. It allows, it embraces, it holds space without judgment. And yet, unconditional love is not the absence of boundaries. It is the presence of clarity, a recognition that love and respect go hand in hand.

As you breathe in, feel the possibility of this love expanding within you. As you exhale, let go of any constraints that have told you love must be earned. Love flows. And you are part of that flow.

The Art of Giving and Receiving

Now, imagine a gentle rhythm, like the ebb and flow of the tide. This is the dance of giving and receiving. Some people give endlessly, pouring out love and energy, yet struggle to accept it in return. Others hesitate to receive, feeling unworthy, hesitant, or even uncomfortable with the vulnerability it requires.

You may notice which role feels more familiar to you. Are you someone who gives freely but hesitates to receive? Or do you hold back, unsure if love is truly meant for you? Just observe. And as you do, recognize that true connection thrives in balance.

Picture a candle's flame. When you use it to light another, your own flame does not diminish. Instead, the room grows brighter. Giving and receiving love is just like that—a mutual enrichment, a shared illumination.

Forgiveness: A Path to Freedom

Now, let's consider forgiveness. Imagine holding a heavy stone. Feel its weight in your hands. This stone represents resentment, anger, or pain from past relationships. You have carried it for so long that you may not even notice its burden anymore.

But what if you could set it down? Not because the hurt never happened, not because you condone it, but because you choose to be free.

Forgiveness is not forgetting. It is releasing. It is choosing to move forward without the weight of the past dragging behind you. As you inhale, feel the possibility of release. As you exhale, imagine setting that stone down, watching it dissolve into the earth, freeing you to walk forward, unburdened.

Cultivating Empathy and Compassion

Empathy is the bridge that connects us. Imagine stepping into another's world, seeing through their eyes, feeling what they feel. Compassion takes this a step further—it is the extension of kindness, even when it is difficult.

Right now, as you read these words, allow yourself to recognize the shared humanity in everyone you meet. Every person has unseen burdens, unspoken hopes. And as you acknowledge this, perhaps a gentle warmth rises within you, a softening, an opening. Compassion is not just for others—it is also for you.

Self-compassion means treating yourself as you would a dear friend. With understanding. With patience. With love. Because when you nurture yourself, you become even more capable of extending that love outward.

The Power of Connection

In the stories that follow, you will witness the dance of relationships—the lessons of unconditional love, the release of forgiveness, and the balance of giving and receiving.

The meditations that accompany these teachings will guide you to deepen these lessons within yourself. You will practice extending compassion—not only to loved ones but to strangers, even those who challenge you. You will learn to receive love as effortlessly as you give it.

Moving Forward

As you read, as you reflect, as you grow, allow these truths to settle within you:

1. *Love flows freely when we open our hearts.*
2. *I give and receive love in balance, allowing connection to flourish.*
3. *I cultivate compassion for myself and others, honoring our shared humanity.*

And perhaps, as you finish reading this, a small shift has already begun within you. A softening. A deepening. A readiness to embrace love, connection, and compassion with fresh eyes and an open heart.

STORY 9 - THE GARDENER MONK: A TEACHING TALE

Introduction: Cultivating the Inner Garden

In a serene monastery perched on a hill in Southeast Asia, a monk named Thich lived with profound simplicity and a heart full of wisdom. To his three students—Mei, Kai, and Lila—he taught that peace did not come from external possessions or achievements but from cultivating an inner garden of calm and contentment. His life was a reflection of this teaching, as he moved through each day with grace, as though living in a park-like state of mind.

Thich's students were each at different stages of their personal journeys. Mei, thoughtful and introspective, often wrestled with self-doubt, stemming from a childhood where she felt overlooked. Kai, practical and ambitious, struggled to reconcile his drive for success with his desire for inner peace, shaped by his urban upbringing. Lila, the youngest, radiated curiosity but grappled with understanding the deeper meaning of her experiences, as her family's frequent relocations left her feeling ungrounded.

The Monk's Morning Meal

The first rays of sunlight danced across the monastery's gardens, where dew sparkled on every leaf. Thich sat cross-legged, a bowl of plain rice and boiled greens in his hands. The rice was grown by villagers, and the greens were harvested from the monastery's own garden. His students gathered around him, observing his ritual of gratitude before eating.

He took each bite slowly, savoring the simplicity. The food was nourishing but plain, designed not to awaken cravings or desires. Thich believed in taking only what was needed to survive each day healthily. By choosing simplicity, he freed himself from the chains of unnecessary want. He did not use consumption to bury emotional pains but sat with them, healing them at their very root. This practice allowed him to eat without attachment, and so his body and mind remained unburdened.

When the meal was over, Thich placed his bowl aside and said softly, "I am now done with consumption. I eat only what does not call out to me in urges—water and simple foods. For that reason, I can say I am done for the day."

Mei, ever curious, asked, "Does that mean you have the rest of the day to yourself, Master?"

Thich chuckled warmly. "No, Mei. That would be thinking only of myself. When my stomach is satisfied, it is time to tend to others."

Kai leaned forward. "But what do you do, Master?"

"I am a gardener," Thich replied.

Lila, tilting her head, asked with a soft smile, "What do you grow?"

Thich's serene smile deepened. "I grow good karma, but more importantly, I grow peace within myself so that I may share it with others."

A State of Needing Nothing

The students followed Thich as he walked along the monastery's winding garden paths. The monk moved with deliberate slowness, as though savoring every step, every breeze, every birdcall. The garden was alive with vibrant colors and the gentle hum of life, mirroring the inner stillness Thich sought to impart. Among the plants were medicinal herbs that the villagers used for healing, symbolizing the harmony between the monastery and the surrounding community.

Kai broke the silence. "Master, how do you remain so calm and content, even when life is difficult?"

Thich stopped and gestured to the surroundings. "Do you feel the stillness of this garden?"

The students nodded.

"This peace exists because the garden needs nothing. It is content as it is. When we put ourselves into a state of needing nothing—not possessions, not recognition, not even others' approval—we, too, create an inner garden like this. In that place, emotions are like soft petals drifting on the breeze, not storms uprooting trees."

He spread his hands, encompassing the trees, flowers, and clear skies. "When you carry a park-like state within you, you naturally feel calm and peaceful, and others sense your harmony, inspiring them to feel the same."

Thich paused and added, "But remember, a garden requires effort. To maintain this inner peace, you must cultivate it daily, as you would water and care for these plants. Neglect allows weeds of worry and discontent to grow."

The Radio and the Boat

Later that day, Thich and his students journeyed to the nearby village, where a farmer waited by a boat filled with manure. The students hesitated at the smell, but Thich approached the farmer with a bow and began helping unload the cargo.

The farmer greeted them with a smile and said, "This manure will feed the rice fields so they bear good fruit."

"Why do you do this, Master?" Mei asked, holding her breath.

Thich smiled. "Manure nourishes the soil, just as life's difficulties nourish the soul. It is unpleasant, but it feeds growth. By embracing it, rather than avoiding it, we create fertile ground for good karma to flourish."

Thich turned to his students and said, "Think of the struggles in your own life. What growth might they be nurturing in you? When we resist challenges, we deny ourselves the chance to grow stronger and wiser."

As they worked, a faint melody from a nearby radio floated through the air. Thich paused, his face lighting up.

"The radio is like the soul," he said. "Its purpose is to broadcast. But what do you think happens if it plays static or discordant noise?"

"It would disturb everyone," Lila replied.

"Precisely," Thich said. "Your inner state is your signal to the world. When you are calm and in harmony, you transmit peace. But if you are filled with greed, anger, or fear, you spread those, too."

Thich gestured to the radio. "Imagine tuning yourself, just as you would adjust this radio. What do you want others to hear from you? What message are you broadcasting?"

Tending to Relationships

Back at the monastery, Thich led the students into the gardens. He began pruning a rose bush, his movements slow and purposeful. Nearby, Mei watched, her brow furrowed as she thought about a recent argument with her sister.

"Every relationship is like a plant," Thich explained. "Some need sunlight—attention and warmth. Others thrive in shade, requiring space and independence. Some need pruning, as we cut away harmful habits or misunderstandings. And some relationships bear fruit, but only if you are patient and nurturing."

The students watched as Thich gently untangled a vine from a nearby shrub. "What happens if you neglect the garden of your relationships?"

"Things wither," Kai said.

"And if you overwater them, demanding too much?" Thich asked.

"They drown," Mei added.

"Exactly," Thich said. "To grow good karma, you must tend to relationships with the same balance and care as a gardener." Mei glanced at the vine Thich had just untangled and resolved to reach out to her sister with kindness and patience. Kai thought about his colleagues at work, realizing he often pushed too hard, and Lila, inspired, decided to call her grandmother, whom she missed deeply.

Thich smiled. "When you nurture a relationship, you not only help it grow, but you also plant seeds of kindness and understanding within yourself. These seeds will blossom into greater harmony in your own life."

A Meditation in the Garden

That evening, Thich guided the students to a quiet clearing. The setting sun painted the sky in hues of orange and gold. Thich sat beneath an ancient banyan tree and invited the students to join him.

"Close your eyes," he instructed, "and picture yourself in a park—not one you can walk through, but one you feel within, where the air is cool, the scent of blooming jasmine surrounds you, and the gentle rustling of leaves brings a sense of calm."
The students settled into stillness as Thich continued.

"In this park, there is no noise, no chaos. Only stillness. You hear the sound of a stream, the rustling of leaves, the song of a bird. Imagine this as your emotional state—a calm, expansive space where nothing is needed and everything is at peace."
The students breathed deeply, their faces softening as the imagery filled their minds.

"Now," Thich said, his voice gentle, "imagine a small boat on the stream. It is carrying manure—your worries, fears, and resentments. Watch it drift away, carried by the current. Feel the soil of your inner park grow richer as the boat empties its load far downstream."

Thich added, "Notice how the stream continues to flow, carrying away all that no longer serves you. This stream is always

available to you, to cleanse and nourish the garden of your heart."
The students remained still, their breathing deep and steady. Each of them visualized the boat and felt lighter, their worries dissolving into the stream.

"Open your eyes," Thich said finally. "Remember: This park is always within you. When you tend it, you walk through life needing nothing, radiating peace to everyone you meet."

Affirmations for Inner Peace

Before the students retired for the night, Thich shared two affirmations:

- *"I carry a beautiful park within me, where stillness and calm flow naturally, and I feel whole and complete in every moment."*

- *"I nourish the soil of my life with kindness, patience, and gratitude, growing beauty in every moment."*

Conclusion: The Blossoming Path

The next day, as the sun rose, Thich began his simple routine anew. He ate his modest meal, walked through the garden, and offered his presence to the world like a gardener tending to his plants.

Through his life, Thich showed that peace is not found in what we consume but in what we cultivate. Living as if in a park, needing nothing, he embodied the beauty of a well-tended soul, offering its blossoms to all who crossed his path.

Discussion Questions
1. What does the metaphor of the garden symbolize for you in your own life?
2. How do you tend to the relationships in your life? Are there any that need more care or balance?
3. In what ways can you practice the concept of "needing nothing" in your daily routine?
4. What does the "radio" metaphor teach you about your inner state and its impact on others?
5. Reflect on the "manure" in your life—challenges or difficulties. How can you use these experiences to nourish your personal growth?
6. How do you "tune" your internal broadcast? What steps can you take to share harmony instead of discord with others?

Dancing Buddha's Quote

"Peace is not an achievement to conquer; it is the garden you tend within your soul. The seeds are patience, kindness, and gratitude, watered daily with love."

STORY 10 – THE BLUE ENERGY OF UNDERSTANDING

Introduction

In a small house near Miami Beach, shaded by swaying palms and the whispers of ocean breezes, a monk named Kaelon lived with his three students: Elias, Clara, and Mateo. They were not ordinary students, nor was Kaelon an ordinary teacher. His lessons often emerged from the mundane, weaving profound truths into everyday experiences. That afternoon, as the late sunlight spilled through the windows, Kaelon called his students into the study, where a bowl of apples rested on the table beside an old radio.

"Today," Kaelon said, "we will explore the dance of perspectives."

His words intrigued his students, but their meaning was unclear. Kaelon's lessons were often layered, unfolding over time like petals of a flower.

The Lesson Begins

Kaelon gestured to the apples. "Take one," he said. Each student reached for an apple, their hands brushing briefly as they chose.

"Close your eyes," Kaelon instructed. "Feel the apple. Notice its weight, texture, and the curve of its skin. Bring it to your nose and inhale its scent."

The students followed his instructions, their minds drawn into the moment. Kaelon's voice was soft yet commanding, a rhythm of calm that seemed to draw them inward, inviting their minds to relax and open. "Now, imagine this apple as a story. Its color, its taste, its journey from the tree to your hand. Each detail holds a fragment of its truth."

Elias spoke first. "It's smooth but firm. There's a coolness to it, like the shade of a tree."

Clara added, "I smell sweetness, but there's a hint of something earthy too."

Mateo hesitated, then said, "I think of the tree it came from, the wind that may have carried its seeds."

Kaelon smiled. "Each of you experiences this apple differently, yet none of you are wrong. Remember this as we continue."

The Radio and the Blue Energy

Kaelon walked over to the old radio and turned its dial. A crackle of static filled the room before settling on a smooth jazz station. The sound wove through the space, changing its mood.

"This radio," Kaelon said, "is like our minds. It tunes into different frequencies, yet the air around us is filled with countless waves we cannot see. Imagine now a transforming blue energy—a radiant, pulsing light—that moves through us and between us. This energy represents understanding."

The students closed their eyes as Kaelon's voice guided them. "See the blue energy flowing like water, weaving into your being and connecting you to one another. Notice how it moves effortlessly, expanding with each breath. As you breathe, let it carry the truth that everyone's perspective is a valid frequency, contributing to a greater harmony."

A Moment of Discord

Later that afternoon, Kaelon took his students for a walk along Miami Beach. The sun sank low, painting the sky in fiery hues as waves lapped at their feet. Mateo, eager to prove his understanding, began arguing with Clara about a philosophical question Kaelon had posed earlier.

"You're missing the point," Mateo insisted. "Kaelon's lesson was about the collective truth, not individual experience."

Clara frowned. "No, it's about seeing value in every perspective, not just the collective. You're twisting his words."

Elias tried to mediate, but his voice was drowned out by the escalating debate.

Kaelon stopped walking and turned to face them. "What do you see when you look at the ocean?" he asked, his tone gentle yet firm.

The students fell silent, confused by the sudden change in topic. Kaelon continued, "Some see peace, others power. Some see adventure, others danger. Who is right?"

They exchanged glances but said nothing.

Kaelon's voice softened. "You are all right, yet none of you hold the entire truth. Like the blue energy we visualized, understanding flows when we honor each perspective, even when it challenges our own. In a way, the world around us is filled with right answers, each shaped by the unique experiences of others. To see the whole truth, we must welcome these differences, weaving them together into a shared wisdom."

The Guided Meditation

That evening, Kaelon led them in a guided meditation under the starlit sky. The ocean's rhythmic waves became their background music.

"Close your eyes," Kaelon began, his voice a soothing balm. "Imagine a glowing blue energy within your chest. With each breath, it grows brighter, radiating outward like sunlight through water."

The students' breathing deepened as they visualized the energy.

"Now," Kaelon continued, "see this energy moving toward the person beside you, merging with their light. Feel the connection—a shared space where differences become strengths. In this space, repeat silently: I honor the truth within myself. I honor the truth within others."

The students repeated the affirmations, their minds calming as the energy united them. Kaelon's voice guided them deeper. "Picture a vast ocean, each wave carrying a perspective, each current holding a shared truth. Feel yourself becoming weightless, floating effortlessly as you trust the flow of understanding to carry you toward clarity and peace."

As the meditation ended, the students opened their eyes. The tension from earlier had dissolved, replaced by a quiet harmony.

Reflection and Closing

The next morning, the students gathered with Kaelon around the breakfast table. The bowl of apples had been replaced with fresh fruit, and the radio played softly in the background.

"What did you learn?" Kaelon asked.

Elias spoke first. "That truth isn't fixed. It's like the ocean, ever-changing and vast."

Clara added, "And that we're not here to hold the right answer but to honor all answers as part of a greater whole."

Mateo nodded. "I see now that cooperation and reframing are essential. We move forward not by proving others wrong but by understanding their innocence and experience."

Kaelon smiled. "Well said. Remember, as we move through life, understanding grows as we welcome diverse perspectives. The speed of understanding is the speed of cooperation, and every step we take together brings us closer to unity."

Affirmation

"I honor the truth within myself and embrace the wisdom in others, knowing that understanding flows where openness begins."

"Like the ocean, I welcome each wave of perspective, knowing that together we create a vast and infinite truth."

Questions for Further Reflection

1. How do you approach situations where you feel your perspective is the only correct one?
2. In what ways can you practice honoring others' truths without diminishing your own?
3. How can visualization techniques, like the blue energy, help you build empathy and connection?
4. Reflect on a recent disagreement. How might reframing the other person's actions as innocent change your perspective?
5.

As the students prepared to leave for their daily tasks, Kaelon turned the radio dial, letting a soft melody fill the room. "Remember," he said, "we are all waves in the same ocean. Each of us carries a truth, and together we form something infinite."

Dancing Buddha's Quote

"We are not the holders of the only truth, but travelers in a sea of truths. To move together, we must dance with understanding, reframing every step as an opportunity to grow in harmony."

Gregory K. Cadotte

STORY 11 - THE WHISPERING TREE

Introduction

The monastery courtyard was bathed in the soft glow of the rising sun. Three students—Mira, Arun, and Leela—sat cross-legged on their yoga mats, facing their teacher, a monk with a serene smile and eyes that seemed to hold the entire universe.

In front of them, the monk placed a wooden tray holding small bowls of rice and steamed vegetables, a simple yet profound offering. The students exchanged puzzled glances but said nothing, sensing there was a deeper lesson hidden in this seemingly ordinary display.

The monk began, his voice like a gentle stream flowing through their minds. "And as you listen now, you may begin to notice a sense of ease settling within you. Today, we speak of the tree, the sprout, and the branches. We will explore how separation is an illusion, how conflict is born from misunderstanding, and how peace arises when we see ourselves as one. But first…" He gestured to the tray. "We start with a story."

Part 1: The Tree's Roots

The monk picked up a grain of rice and held it between his fingers.

"Once," he began, "there was a mighty tree, vast and ancient. It began as a single sprout, growing upward with determination and grace. Over time, it divided into countless branches. Each branch stretched in its own direction, reaching for light, unaware of the others.

One day, two neighboring branches began to argue. 'You're blocking my sunlight!' cried one. 'And you're stealing my water!' retorted the other.

The tree listened, amused, for it knew a truth the branches had forgotten: they were part of the same whole. The water flowed through the same roots. The sunlight nourished the same trunk. Yet the branches, in their different positions, mistook their individuality for separation.

Their leaves, too, fretted as autumn approached. 'We are falling! We will die!' they whispered. But the tree knew better. When the leaves fell, they returned to the earth, nourishing the roots from which they came. The tree felt no loss—only transformation."

The students listened, enraptured. Arun raised his hand. "Master, if the branches are all one, why do they quarrel?"

The monk's smile widened. "And as you think about that, you might begin to realize… they forget. They see themselves as apart, not as a part. And so they suffer. But if they were to pause, to remember the time before they stretched out in different directions, they would feel their unity once more. And so can we. When you find yourself in conflict, return to that place within you where there was no division, where you were whole, and let that memory guide you back to peace."

Part 2: Rice, Vegetables, and the Illusion of Separation

The monk picked up a bowl of rice and a piece of steamed vegetable, holding them thoughtfully.

"Now, consider this rice and vegetable. One is grain, one is plant. If the rice argued with the vegetable over which was more important, would it make sense? They are different, yet together they create a nourishing meal. And as you reflect on this, you might begin to sense how everything is connected in its own way."

Mira giggled. "But Master, it's so obvious they're meant to be enjoyed together."

"Exactly," the monk said. "And yet, humans do this all the time. We argue over who is more deserving of sunshine, more entitled to water, forgetting that we are all part of the same tree. Even when the leaf falls, it is still the tree, simply in another form."

Leela frowned, her gaze distant. "But what about spirits, Master? What are they in this metaphor?"

The monk's voice softened. "Ah, spirits. They are the whispers of the roots and limbs, moving in ways we cannot perceive. They are not separate from us; they are the rustlings of the great tree of life. What we call 'spirits' are simply parts of ourselves that we do not yet understand. And as you hear these words, you might begin to feel an awareness growing inside you, a knowing that has always been there."

Part 3: Guided Meditation: The Tree Within

The monk gestured for the students to close their eyes.

"Sit tall, like a tree," he instructed. "Feel the ground beneath you, solid and steady, like roots anchoring you to the earth. And as you breathe in deeply now, you may begin to sense a gentle strength rising within you. With each inhale, imagine drawing water and nutrients up from the soil, nourishing your body and soul.

Now, visualize a sprout emerging from the earth. See it grow, reaching toward the sunlight. Its stem divides, forming branches. Each branch stretches outward, finding its place, yet remaining connected to the trunk.

Notice the leaves on the branches, vibrant and green. They sway in the breeze, hearing whispers of their impermanence. Feel their worry. And now... shift your perspective—see the tree. See how the leaf is never separate from the tree. When it falls, it is not lost; its consciousness still in the tree and its body transforms, returning to the earth, feeding the roots.

Finally, hear the whispers of the roots and limbs. They are alive, moving, speaking in ways beyond your perception. And as you listen, you may begin to realize... you are the tree, the branch, the leaf, the root. You are never apart. You are always a part."

The students' breathing slowed. Their bodies softened, their faces serene.

Part 4: The Quarrel of Branches

After a moment of silence, the monk spoke again.

"Imagine now that you are a branch of this great tree. You see another branch growing toward the sunlight you thought was yours. And as you notice this, how do you feel?"

Mira hesitated. "Jealous. Angry, maybe."

"Good," the monk said. "Now look deeper. Realize that this other branch draws water from the same roots as you. Its growth strengthens the tree, and so it strengthens you. And as you let that thought settle, how do you feel now?"

"Relieved," Leela whispered.

"At peace," Arun added.

The monk nodded. "And as you continue to reflect, you might find yourself remembering... when you understand that what seems separate is truly one, you free yourself from suffering. And in those moments of conflict, simply return to the root, return to the place before you thought you were apart, and you will find your way home."

Affirmations

"I am part of the great tree of life, connected to all and never alone."

"I release the illusion of separation and embrace the truth of unity."

"With each breath, I deepen my connection to the whole."

Questions for Further Discussion

1. Why do we often see ourselves as separate from others,

even when we share the same roots?
2. How can understanding the tree metaphor help us resolve conflicts in our lives?
3. Reflect on a time when you felt connected to something greater than yourself. What did that feel like?
4. In what ways can you practice seeing yourself as part of a greater whole?

Conclusion

As the sun climbed higher in the sky, the students bowed to the monk. They gathered their yoga mats and walked to the dining hall, their steps lighter and their hearts fuller.

The monk remained under the tree, watching its branches sway in the gentle breeze. And as he sat in stillness, he smiled, knowing that within each student, a quiet understanding was taking root, growing stronger with every breath.

Dancing Buddha's Quote

"The branches may stretch in different directions, but the roots remain one. To remember our connection is to remember peace."

STORY 12 – THE PRESENT MOMENT -LOVE WHERE IT BELONGS

Introduction

The Himalayan valley was quiet except for the soft rustle of wind through the trees. The morning sun spilled golden light over the snow-capped peaks, melting frost from the grass and bringing the world to life in shades of green and gold. Near the edge of the mountain, nestled within a grove of ancient oaks, sat a modest monastery. Its wooden beams gleamed with care, and prayer flags fluttered in the breeze, their vibrant reds, blues, and yellows sending whispered blessings into the air.

Inside the monastery courtyard, Master Suriya gathered his students. Sometimes it was one. Sometimes it was many. Today, there were five: Arun, a restless dreamer who carried his love in the future; Meera, a grieving widow whose love lingered in the past; Jia, an artist searching for inspiration in the present; and two travelers, Mira and Naveen, strangers to the group but drawn by curiosity and the promise of wisdom.

Master Suriya stood under a maple tree, its crimson leaves falling like whispers to the earth. He radiated a calm that seemed to expand through the courtyard, a calm that spoke without words. His robes, shimmering in shades of saffron and maroon, caught the sunlight, amplifying his presence.

"Today," Suriya said, his voice like the steady flow of water, "we will talk about love—what it is, where it lives, and why it often feels so far away."

Section 1: Love in the Past and Future

"Tell me," Suriya continued, his gaze resting on each student in turn, "where does your love live?"

Arun spoke first. "In the future," he said. "I love what I'm building, what I want to achieve. But it always feels like I'm chasing something I can't catch."

Meera hesitated, then said, "Mine is in the past—with my husband. He's gone now, but my love for him stays there. And sometimes, it feels like... pain."

Jia added softly, "I think my love is here, but sometimes I feel distracted—like I can't hold on to it."

Suriya nodded. "You've each named something important. Love, when misplaced, changes its nature. In the past, it becomes longing, regret, or sorrow. In the future, it turns into worry, pressure, and fear. Only in the present does love feel like itself—peaceful, whole, and alive."

He paused, letting the weight of his words settle. "But so often, we leave our love behind or cast it ahead. We scatter it.

And when it is scattered, we feel restless, burdened, or lost."

Suriya bent down and picked up a small, smooth stone. He held it up for the group to see. "Imagine this stone is your love. When you place it in the past, how does it feel?"

Meera's voice was barely above a whisper. "Heavy. Like something I can't lift."

Suriya placed the stone in her hand. "And when it is in the future?"

Arun sighed. "Like it's slipping away—like I'm never enough to reach it."

Suriya nodded. "And when it is here, in the present?"

Jia closed her eyes, her hand moving to her chest. "It feels warm. Like it belongs."

Suriya smiled. "Exactly. Love, when placed in the present, transforms. It becomes what it was always meant to be. The Buddha, who embodied pure love, understood this. He placed his love here, in this moment. And when people were near him, they felt it as though it were their own."

Section 2: A Lesson from the River

Suriya gestured for the group to follow him, leading them down a narrow path toward a river that sparkled in the morning light. The water reflected the colors of the surrounding forest—emerald greens and deep browns—and the occasional flash of orange leaves drifting on the surface.

"Water teaches us about love," Suriya said as they approached the riverbank. "It flows where it is needed, always present, always renewing itself. But what happens if the water is blocked—trapped in the past or rushing too far ahead?"

"It stagnates," Jia said.

"Or it dries up," added Naveen.

Suriya picked up a handful of river stones and handed one to each student. "Hold this stone tightly," he said. "Squeeze it as if it were your love, stuck in the past or straining toward the future. How does it feel?"

"It hurts," Meera said, wincing.

"Now," Suriya continued, "place it in the water."

One by one, the students released their stones into the river. The water rippled gently as the stones disappeared beneath the surface.

"And how does it feel now?" Suriya asked.

Meera smiled for the first time. "Lighter. Like it's part of something larger."

Section 3: Guided Meditation

Later, back at the monastery, Suriya invited the students to the meditation hall. The room was serene, lit by the soft glow of candles and the golden hues of the setting sun. Cushions in shades of burgundy and saffron were arranged in a circle.

"Sit comfortably," Suriya instructed, his voice a steady rhythm that seemed to echo in the stillness. "Close your eyes and take a deep breath. Feel the air as it moves in and out of your body, connecting you to this moment."

The students obeyed, their breathing slowing.

"Now," Suriya continued, "imagine a thread of light, golden and warm, resting in your heart. This thread is your love. Notice where it stretches. Does it reach behind you, into the past? Or ahead, into the future? See it clearly."

Meera's lips trembled. "It's behind me," she whispered.

"Gently," Suriya said, "gather that thread. Draw it back into your heart. Feel how it softens, warms, and begins to glow brighter. Notice how it feels when your love is here, in the present—free, whole, and alive."

The room grew quiet as the students sat with their love gathered into the present. Arun sighed, his shoulders dropping. Jia smiled, a tear slipping down her cheek.

Section 4: The Color of Love

After the meditation, Suriya asked, "If love in the present were a color, what would it be?"

"Gold," Jia said, "like the light in the hall."

"Blue," Arun said, "like the sky when it's clear."

"Green," Meera said, her voice steady. "Like spring."

Suriya nodded. "When love is in the present, it takes on every color. It is vibrant, alive, and whole. Remember this: when you feel weighed down by the past or anxious about the future, ask yourself, 'What color is my love right now?' Bring it back to the present, where it shines brightest."

Conclusion

The students left the monastery that day transformed. Meera found peace in her memories, no longer burdened by loss. Arun let go of the pressure to chase a future that felt out of reach. Jia felt her creativity rekindle, inspired by the colors of love she now saw everywhere.

Master Suriya stood at the edge of the monastery, watching them go. The sun dipped low in the sky, casting hues of gold and crimson across the valley. He knew their journeys were just beginning, but they now carried the greatest gift: love, placed where it belongs—in the present.

Affirmations

"I bring my love into the present, where it feels whole, peaceful, and alive."

"In this moment, I choose to love fully and freely."

Questions for Further Discussion

1. How does it feel when your love is focused on the past? The future?
2. What practices can help you bring your love back into the present?
3. If love were a color for you right now, what would it be, and why?
4. How can you let go of love that feels misplaced or scattered?
5. How can you share present-focused love with others in your life?

Dancing Buddha's Quote

"Love, like the sun, can only shine in the present. When scattered across time, it is dimmed. But here, in this moment, it burns brightly, warming all it touches."

STORY 13 – THE PATH BEYOND THE ARROWS

Introduction

In a tranquil mountain monastery, nestled among cherry blossoms and pine trees, life moved to the gentle rhythm of the seasons. Overlooking a softly singing river, the monastery was a sanctuary of peace and wisdom, where moments deepened, and the practice of being present was both art and life.

Here lived Master Kaien, whose calm presence radiated a stillness that drew people to him like moths to a flame. His three students—Riku, an ambitious seeker with a restless heart; Mei, a thoughtful artist full of questions; and Taro, a quiet observer of life's mysteries—shared their days in study and practice under his guidance.

One morning, Mei's beloved cat, Sora, went missing. The students searched the gardens, the halls, and even the forest beyond the monastery's gates, calling out for the elusive feline. By midday, they returned empty-handed, their faces clouded with worry and frustration.

What Is Different About You?

"Master Kaien," Riku said, his voice tinged with impatience, "Sora is gone, and yet you sit here so calmly. Why are you so different from us? Why don't you seem concerned?"

Kaien looked up from the smooth stone he had been turning in his hands. His gaze was steady, his expression serene. He smiled gently and said, "What is different about me?"

"Yes," Mei added, her voice soft but filled with curiosity. "What is it that makes you so calm when we feel so restless?"

Kaien placed the stone down and folded his hands in his lap. His voice carried a profound stillness. "What is different about me is this: I am on no journey, and for that reason, I am always here with you."

The students exchanged puzzled glances.

"What does that mean?" Mei asked, her brow furrowed.

Kaien gestured for them to follow him. "Let me show you."

The Arrows of Life

In the study, Kaien placed a blank sheet of paper on the table and handed each student a pen. "Draw arrows," he said. "Draw as many as you like, pointing in any direction."

The students complied. Soon the paper was a chaotic sea of arrows, pointing left, right, up, down, and diagonally.

Kaien held up the paper. "Now," he said, "examine this from above. What do you see? How does it feel?"

"It feels chaotic," Mei said. "There's no sense to it."

"It's overwhelming," Riku added. "There are too many directions to follow."

Kaien nodded, setting the paper down. "Now," he continued, "close your eyes. Imagine you are one of the arrows. Feel yourself moving in its direction. What happens?"

The students followed his instructions.

Riku spoke first, his voice tight. "Some arrows are pushing against me. It's frustrating."

Mei's tone was thoughtful. "Some arrows are with me. That feels easier, but even then, I can only see the path ahead. It's limiting."

Taro, ever the quiet one, said, "Some arrows don't matter much, but they still shape the way I move. It feels... indirect."

Kaien smiled. "This is how most live, moving through life as arrows, tied to directions and journeys. Some are with you, some against, but all of them keep you tethered. What happens when you let go of being an arrow?"

The End of Journeys

The students opened their eyes, the paper before them taking on a new meaning.

"But Master," Riku asked, "how do we live without journeys? Isn't life full of paths we must follow?"

Kaien's voice was calm and rhythmic. "End the journeys of

the flesh—those fueled by addictions and compulsions. End the journeys of fear and desire—those that tie your heart to endless seeking. And most importantly, let unconditional love end many journeys. Love that asks nothing of you, demands nothing of others, allows things to move at their own pace and in their own way. In that love, the need to chase or resist dissolves."

The students sat in reflective silence, the depth of his words settling over them.

"Unconditional love creates stillness," Kaien continued. "Even as you move physically, you can rest emotionally. You become like a mountain river—flowing, yet calm. When I tell you I am always here with you, it is because I am needless. I have nothing to take, no demands to impose. I am content, open, and at peace."

Guided Meditation: Rising Above the Arrows

Kaien led the students into the garden, where the golden light of the setting sun bathed the world in warmth. The koi pond glistened, its surface reflecting the sky.

"Sit," Kaien instructed, his voice soft yet steady. "Close your eyes and breathe deeply. Feel the ground beneath you, solid and unwavering. Hear the river's song and let it guide your breath."

The students settled into the rhythm, their breaths slow and steady.

"Now," Kaien continued, "imagine yourself as one of the arrows on the page. Feel the pull of directions, the tug of desires, the weight of fears. Notice how these movements shape you."

He paused, letting the image settle.

"Now imagine yourself rising above, like a bird soaring over the arrows. Feel the freedom as you lift higher. From this view, the arrows are just patterns below. They do not control you. You are not bound by them. You are the sky in which they exist."

Kaien's voice softened, carrying them deeper into the visualization. "Say silently: 'I am here. I am now. I am enough.' With each breath, let the truth of these words grow within you."

As the students meditated, the garden seemed to still, the koi gliding effortlessly beneath the water's surface.

The Return of Sora

When they opened their eyes, there was Sora, sitting serenely by Mei's side as if she had never been lost at all.

Kaien smiled. "What we seek often appears when we stop searching."

The students laughed, their hearts lighter than they had been all day.

Conclusion

That evening, as stars filled the sky, the monastery was alive with quiet joy. The students carried their master's teachings within them—not as arrows pointing toward distant goals, but as the calm presence of unconditional love that welcomed life exactly as it was.

In that love, they discovered the infinite, and the world became both still and alive with endless possibilities.

Affirmations

"I release the need to chase or resist; in stillness, I find peace, and in presence, I am free."

"Like the sky above the arrows, I rise beyond fear and desire, embracing the boundless love that already exists within me."

Questions for Further Discussion

1. What arrows or directions do you feel pulled by in your life?
2. How can unconditional love help you let go of fear and desire?
3. What does it mean to rise above the arrows and find stillness within movement?
4. How can you apply the affirmation "I am whole, I am free, I am love" to daily life?

Dancing Buddha's Quote

"When we stop chasing the arrows of life, we find the space to be. In that space, love moves freely, and all things find their way."

STORY 14 - SLAVE OR MASTER OF LOVE

Introduction

High in the Himalayan mountains, a monastery known as the Sanctuary of Light stood as a refuge for seekers of wisdom. Here, Master Ravi guided students not only to enlightenment but to profound self-discovery. Among his students were Sita, a healer with a compassionate heart; Kamal, a sharp and ambitious thinker; and Theo, a quiet traveler seeking clarity.

One crisp morning, Master Ravi called his students to the meditation hall. As the golden light of dawn filled the room, his calm voice resonated like the steady flow of a stream. "Today," he began, "we will explore the states of love—its chains and its liberation. Love can enslave you, or it can free you. But before you can master love, you must first become its student."

The students listened intently, intrigued by his words.

"Let us begin by understanding what it means to be a slave of love," Ravi said, motioning for them to follow him.

The Bondage of Love: The Weight of Stones

Master Ravi led them to the monastery courtyard, where a clay pot sat beside a pile of stones and a jug of water. Kneeling by the pot, he picked up a stone.

"This pot," he said, "represents your heart. It has space to hold love, like water. But watch what happens when you add stones."

He placed the stone in the pot and poured water in until it reached the brim. "Now the pot holds both water and the stone," Ravi said. "The stone represents attachment, and the water represents free love. When you cling to something—a person, an expectation, or a fear—you add a stone to your heart."

He continued placing stones into the pot, one by one. The water overflowed, spilling onto the ground. Finally, the pot could hold no more water. It was heavy, weighed down by stones.

"This is the heart of a slave of love," Ravi said. "Every stone you carry is an attachment—possessiveness, jealousy, the fear of loss. When you are a slave of love, you cling tightly to these stones, believing they are love itself. But the more stones you carry, the less space you have for love to flow freely."

Kamal frowned. "But Master, isn't attachment part of love? How can we love without holding on?"

Master Ravi nodded. "Attachment can feel like love, but it is not. When attachment binds your love, you fear its loss, and that fear enslaves you. You become chained to the very thing you desire, unable to move freely."

He picked up another pot, this one already full of stones, and poured water into it. The water splashed and spilled everywhere, unable to settle inside. "This is the cost of being a slave of love.

Even when love is offered to you, there is no room to receive it. It spills away, wasted."

Sita, her face troubled, asked, "Master, what can we do? How do we stop being slaves of love?"

"To free yourself, you must first become a student of love," Ravi replied. "A student observes, questions, and learns. Examine the stones you carry. What attachments weigh you down? Why do you cling to them? Only through understanding can you begin to let them go."

Becoming a Student of Love

Master Ravi led the students to a shaded grove near the river. They sat in a circle, the soft rustling of leaves and the murmuring water creating a peaceful rhythm.

"To become a student of love," Ravi said, "you must observe the states of your heart. When you feel love, ask yourself: Is this love pure and expansive, or is it bound by attachment? Am I seeking to give or to possess? Am I free, or am I clinging?"

The students fell silent, reflecting on his words.

"Now," Ravi continued, "consider this: When you love someone or something, do you hold tightly out of fear? Do you expect something in return? These are signs of slavery. A student of love recognizes these patterns and learns to release them."

He paused, then said, "The path to mastery begins here. When you understand love as a river, not a possession, you can let it flow freely. Only then can you become its master."

The Stranger's Dilemma

As they discussed the lesson, a man from a nearby village approached. His face was lined with worry, and he carried a basket of goods that seemed to weigh heavily on him. Bowing deeply, he said, "Master Ravi, please help me. My son refuses to marry the woman I have chosen for him. I act out of love, but he says I am controlling his life. How can love bring such pain?"

Master Ravi handed the man a stone. "Hold this tightly," he said. "This stone represents your love for your son."

The man gripped the stone, confusion clouding his face.

"Now imagine your love is like the water in the pot," Ravi said. "When you hold onto the stone, you leave less space for love to flow. Your grip does not free your son; it only binds you both."

The man's grip loosened. "What should I do, Master?"

"Release the stone," Ravi said softly. "Let your love flow like water—free of control, free of fear. Give your son the space to choose his path, and you will find that your love becomes lighter, purer."

The man dropped the stone. His shoulders lifted, as if a great weight had been removed. "Thank you, Master," he said, bowing before leaving.

Guided Meditation: The River of Love

That evening, Master Ravi brought the students to the riverbank. The setting sun painted the water in hues of gold and crimson, and the gentle current whispered of freedom.

"Sit," Ravi instructed, motioning to the soft grass. The students closed their eyes, following his guidance.

"Breathe deeply," he said, his voice low and rhythmic. "Feel the earth beneath you, steady and unshaken. Hear the river's flow, constant and free."

The students' breathing slowed, matching the rhythm of the water.

"Now," Ravi continued, "imagine that you are holding a stone. This stone represents an attachment—a fear, expectation, or desire you cling to in the name of love. Feel its weight in your hand."

Sita imagined the weight of her need to protect her patients. Kamal thought of his desire for approval, and Theo pictured his longing for a lost connection.

"Step closer to the river," Ravi said. "See its flow—effortless, expansive, infinite. When you are ready, release the stone into the current. Watch as it sinks and becomes part of the river's flow."

The students visualized the act of release, a deep sense of peace washing over them as if the river had carried away their burdens.

"Repeat after me," Ravi said:

'I release what binds me and let love flow freely.'

'I am the master of my love, not its slave.'"

Their voices carried over the water, steady and serene.

"Now," Ravi concluded, "imagine the river expanding, flowing beyond the mountains and into the sea. Let your love stretch without boundary, touching all things. Feel its infinite nature within you."

Conclusion

In the days that followed, the students practiced observing their hearts. Kamal noticed the weight of his need for validation and began letting go. Sita softened her protective instincts, learning to care without fear. Theo, once preoccupied with regret, embraced the present moment with a lighter heart.

Master Ravi watched their progress with quiet satisfaction. "Remember," he told them one evening, "you are always a student of love. Observe it, learn from it, and let it guide you. When you release the stones, you are no longer a slave to love. You become its master."

Questions for Further Discussion

1. What stones are you holding in your heart?
2. How can being a student of love help you release attachments?
3. How does the imagery of the pot and river help you understand the nature of love?
4. What does it mean to love without fear or possession?

Dancing Buddha's Quote

"Love, when bound, is a chain. Love, when learned, is a teacher. Love, when free, is a river that nourishes all."

STORY 15 - THE ART OF EMOTIONAL NOURISHMENT

Introduction

In a monastery nestled in a lush valley, Master Dhava guided his students, Amar and Kavi, on the art of living with emotional balance. Outside the monastery, the world was rife with unrest—villages squabbled, and travelers brought tales of conflict. Yet within the monastery walls, Dhava sought to teach his students how to walk through such a world without carrying its burdens.

One morning, as the golden light of dawn streamed through the mountains, Dhava called Amar and Kavi to the meditation hall. The faint scent of incense filled the air, mingling with the soft murmur of a nearby stream.

"Today," Dhava began, "I will teach you about nourishment. Not of the body, but of the heart and mind."

The students exchanged curious glances. Amar, always eager, leaned forward. "What do you mean, Master?"

Dhava gestured for them to follow him to the monastery garden. There, he plucked a ripe peach from a tree and held it up. "When we eat, we do not consume the stem, the seed, or the pit. We take only the flesh—the part that nourishes us—and leave the rest behind. Why do we do this?"

"To avoid harm," Kavi said thoughtfully.

"To gain strength," Amar added.

Dhava nodded. "Exactly. Now consider this: every interaction, every moment, is like this peach. Some parts nourish the soul, while others can harm it. Wisdom lies in taking what strengthens you and leaving the rest behind. Repeat after me: *'I take only what nourishes me and leave the rest behind.'*"

The students repeated the affirmation, and Amar felt his initial confusion begin to clear.

The Traveler's Anger

Later that day, the trio walked to a nearby village to gather supplies. On the road, they encountered a weary traveler, his clothes dusty and his expression stormy. As he approached, his voice was sharp and impatient.

"Can't you monks walk faster? You block the path as if the world owes you its time!" he snapped.

Amar bristled, his fists clenching. "How dare he speak to us like that?" he whispered to Kavi.

Kavi, calmer but still unsettled, muttered, "It's best to ignore him."

Dhava, however, stepped forward and bowed slightly to the traveler. "Forgive us, friend. The path is wide, and you are free to pass. May your journey bring you peace."

The traveler muttered something incoherent and hurried on, leaving a tense silence behind.

"Master," Amar said, his voice tight, "why did you let him insult us?"

Dhava smiled gently. "Did he insult us, Amar? Or did he reveal the turbulence within his own heart?"

Amar frowned but said nothing.

Dhava continued, "Tell me, what have you taken from this moment?"

"I've taken offense," Amar admitted.

"And you, Kavi?"

"I've taken caution," Kavi replied. "His anger reminds me to guard myself."

Dhava nodded. "Both are seeds—offense and caution. But are they nourishing? Or have you swallowed the pit instead of the fruit?"

The students looked at him, puzzled.

"The traveler's anger was not ours to carry," Dhava said. "He offered it freely, but we need not accept it. What we can take is the lesson: compassion. He is weighed down by his struggles, and we have the strength to walk lightly. Take this understanding and leave the rest behind. Repeat after me: *'I walk lightly, carrying only what serves my growth.'*"

The students repeated the words, and Amar felt his clenched fists relax.

The Farmer's Generosity

That evening, they visited a farmer who often donated food to the monastery. The farmer greeted them warmly, handing them a basket of fresh vegetables. "These are from my best harvest," he said. "I hope they nourish your spirits as they have nourished mine."

Kavi smiled. "Such generosity is rare. It fills me with hope."

Amar nodded. "It makes me grateful."

Dhava observed quietly. On the walk back, he asked, "What have you taken from the farmer's gesture?"

"Gratitude," Amar said.

"Hope," Kavi replied.

Dhava smiled. "Good. But remember, even in moments of kindness, seeds can remain—seeds of attachment or expectation. If you begin to believe that the world owes you kindness, you plant a seed that may grow into disappointment."

Amar frowned. "So even good moments can carry harm?"

"No, Amar," Dhava said. "They carry lessons. Take the nourishment of gratitude and hope, but leave behind expectation. Let your heart remain open, free to embrace each moment as it comes."

The Storm and the Calm

One stormy night, as rain lashed against the monastery walls, Dhava gathered his students in the hall. Thunder growled like an angry beast, and the lamp on the altar flickered in the wind's draft.

"This storm," Dhava began, "is like the emotions of the world. Many are swept away by its force, overwhelmed by its noise. But you can learn to stand firm."

"How, Master?" Kavi asked.

Dhava placed a small lamp on the floor, its flame wavering but holding steady. "This lamp stands in the storm, but it does not fight the wind. It bends, flickers, but does not falter. So must your spirit be. Do not resist the storm, but do not let it consume you."

Amar watched the flame, his face filled with wonder. "But how do we remain so steady?"

"By digesting the storm," Dhava said. "Take what strengthens you—the challenge, the resilience it awakens—and leave behind what does not yet serve you. The fear, the anger—these are unripe fruit. Let them be. They will nourish you in time."

Guided Meditation: Emotional Nourishment

Master Dhava led his students into the garden, where the rain had softened to a gentle mist. The air was cool, carrying the scent of damp earth and the faint sweetness of blossoms stirred by the breeze. The clouds overhead parted slightly, revealing a sliver of moonlight that bathed the garden in a silvery glow.

"Sit," Dhava instructed, motioning to a soft patch of grass under a peach tree. The students complied, crossing their legs and resting their hands on their knees. The grass was cool and slightly damp, grounding them in the present moment.

Dhava settled before them, his posture as steady as the trunk of the tree behind him. "Close your eyes," he said, his voice low and calming, like the first notes of a lullaby. "Feel the ground beneath you. Let its support remind you that you are connected to something larger, something steady and unchanging."

Amar and Kavi closed their eyes. Dhava continued, his words slow and deliberate. "Picture yourself holding a peach in your hand. Feel its weight resting in your palm. Notice its texture—the slight fuzz on the skin, the curve of its shape. Imagine the color: a deep, warm gold tinged with red, as if kissed by the sun."

The students' breathing slowed, their bodies softening as they followed his words. "Now, imagine biting into it," Dhava said, his tone becoming softer still. "Feel the juices on your lips, the sweetness filling your mouth. Let the taste spread, nourishing you with its richness."

The imagery pulled Amar and Kavi deeper into the experience. They could almost feel the peach, taste its sweetness, and sense the joy it brought.

"Now," Dhava continued, "you reach the pit. It is hard, unyielding, and bitter. Notice it, acknowledge its presence, but do not hold onto it. Let it fall from your hand to the ground. The earth will take it back, to grow or dissolve as it chooses. You have taken what nourishes you; the rest is not yours to carry."

The students' breaths became deeper, slower. A light breeze rustled the leaves above them, as if echoing the release Dhava described.

"Feel this truth in your body," Dhava said. "With each breath, you take in what nourishes you: calm, strength, clarity. And with each exhale, you release what does not serve you: tension, anger, fear. Imagine the exhale carrying these burdens away, scattering them like petals in the wind."

For a moment, there was only the sound of their breathing, synchronized with the rhythm of the garden around them—the faint trickle of water from a nearby stream, the chirp of a cricket hidden in the grass, the occasional patter of a remaining raindrop falling from the leaves.

"Now," Dhava said, his voice like the faint glow of the moon, "repeat after me:

'*I take only what nourishes me and leave the rest behind.*'"

Amar and Kavi spoke softly, their voices steady and sure. "I take only what nourishes me and leave the rest behind."

"Good," Dhava said. "Now, another: *I walk lightly, carrying only what serves my growth.*'"

They repeated in unison, their voices a little stronger now.

"I walk lightly, carrying only what serves my growth."

Dhava let the silence linger for a moment, allowing the affirmations to settle deeply into their hearts.

"Before you open your eyes," Dhava said, "imagine yourself walking through the world. See the people, the chaos, the noise. Now, picture yourself like a tree, rooted and unshaken. The winds blow, but you remain steady. The storms rage, but you stand firm. The sun shines, and you grow. You carry with you only what strengthens you, leaving the rest to pass by."

Amar felt a deep calm settle in his chest, as if a weight he hadn't realized he was carrying had been lifted. Kavi felt lighter too, as though the very air around him had become clearer, brighter.

Dhava's voice, now just above a whisper, brought them back. "When you are ready, open your eyes."

The students opened their eyes slowly, blinking at the soft light of the moon and the gentle sway of the peach tree's branches above them. The garden seemed more vivid now, each detail sharper, each sound more harmonious.

"Do you feel it?" Dhava asked. "The lightness, the clarity?"

"Yes, Master," Kavi said, his voice soft but steady.

"I feel... free," Amar added, his words carrying a note of awe.

Dhava smiled, his gaze warm and knowing. "This is the gift of nourishment—not just for the body, but for the spirit. When you take only what serves you and leave the rest, you are free to walk lightly in the world, unburdened and strong."

The three sat quietly for a few more moments, the peace of the garden settling into their bones. The moon, now fully visible, cast its light over them, as if blessing the lesson learned.

Walking Through the World

Months later, Amar and Kavi walked through a bustling marketplace. They saw a man shouting at a merchant, a child laughing with a stray dog, and a beggar offering a wooden trinket to passersby.

"Look at this place," Amar said. "It's a storm of emotions."

"Yes," Kavi replied, "but we can take what nourishes us and leave the rest. The laughter of the child, the generosity of the beggar—these are the fruits. The anger of the man is only a seed we are not yet ready to plant."

Dhava, walking behind them, smiled. "You have learned well. To walk through this world and remain whole is the greatest art. It is not about avoiding the storm but dancing within it, taking only what makes you stronger."

The students felt a deep peace settle within them. The world's chaos remained, but they were no longer burdened by its weight.

Affirmations

"I take only what nourishes me and leave the rest behind."

"I walk lightly, carrying only what serves my growth."

Questions for Further Discussion

1. How can we identify what nourishes us emotionally and what doesn't?
2. What are some techniques to "digest the storm" of emotions in daily life?
3. Have you ever carried someone else's anger? How did it affect you?
4. How can affirmations help in moments of emotional overwhelm?

Dancing Buddha's Quote

"The fruit nourishes, the seed grows, and the pit falls away. So too must we take from the world what strengthens us, plant what serves others, and leave the rest to the earth."

Gregory K. Cadotte

STORY 16 - EXPANDED LOVE IS PEACE

Introduction

In a quiet monastery nestled among misty hills, Master Ananda, a serene monk whose presence exuded calm, guided his students with wisdom that felt both profound and playful. Among his students were Ravi, who wrestled with doubt; Priya, who pondered deeply; and Arun, whose impatience often clouded his understanding.

One morning, beneath the shade of a sprawling banyan tree, Ravi voiced a question that had been troubling him. "Master, how can loving *everything* lead to peace? Doesn't love lose its depth when spread too thin?" To Ravi, the idea felt extreme.

Master Ananda's eyes twinkled with a knowing smile. "Ah, Ravi. Let us explore this together. Love, when confined to one thing, can bring conflict and fear. But love, when expanded, brings harmony and peace. Come, let me show you."

The Bowl and the Drop

Ananda led his students to a nearby stream, carrying a simple clay bowl. Cupping his hands, he let a single droplet fall into the bowl. "This is how most begin their journey," he said. "Focused on one small object of their love. What happens if this drop evaporates?"

Priya, ever thoughtful, replied, "Then the love is gone."

Ananda nodded. "And when the object of our love is gone, we often feel loss, fear, and conflict." He then filled the bowl to its brim with water. "Now, the bowl overflows. When you expand your love, it no longer clings to one thing but embraces everything it touches. Love, when shared broadly, does not deplete—it multiplies."

Arun, curious but skeptical, asked, "But can too much love cause us to lose focus? Doesn't it overflow wastefully?"

"Let us see," Ananda said, motioning them to follow.

The Sparrow's Song

As they walked through the forest, they heard a sparrow's panicked chirping. Tangled in a thorny bush, the bird struggled to free itself.

"Help it," Ananda instructed.

Ravi hesitated, fearing the sharp thorns, but Priya stepped forward without hesitation. She gently untangled the sparrow, cradling it in her hands before releasing it into the sky. The bird's song turned jubilant as it flew away.

"What did you feel?" Ananda asked Priya.

"Warmth and joy," she replied, smiling softly.

Ananda turned to Ravi. "Do you see? Love does not diminish when shared. It grows. When we love only one thing, we risk clinging and creating division. But when we love all things, even briefly, we nurture connection and peace."

Ravi nodded, his resistance beginning to fade. "I felt it too, Master. A connection."

"And that," Ananda said, "is the path to peace."

The Merchant's Dilemma

Further down the path, they came across a merchant sitting by the roadside, weeping. His cart had overturned, spilling pots of oil and sacks of grain onto the dirt. Arun's first instinct was to keep walking, but Ananda stopped.

Without a word, Ananda began helping the merchant gather his scattered goods. Seeing this, Priya and Ravi joined in. Even Arun, after a moment's hesitation, knelt to assist. Together, they salvaged what they could, uprighted the cart, and reassured the merchant.

As they walked away, Ananda asked, "How did it feel to help?"

"It felt good," Ravi admitted. "But why did we help him? We gained nothing."

Ananda chuckled. "Love asks for nothing in return, yet it gives endlessly. When we love only one thing, we may create barriers to others. But when we act from love without limits, we dissolve those barriers and invite peace."

The Broken Jar

Back at the monastery, Ravi accidentally dropped a clay jar he was carrying. It shattered into countless pieces. Embarrassed, he muttered apologies, but Ananda picked up a shard and held it to the light.

"Do you think your love for this jar is wasted because it broke?"

"I... I don't know," Ravi said, his voice heavy with guilt.

Ananda smiled. "Love, when focused on a single object, often leads to fear of loss. But love, like light, is never wasted. The jar is gone, but the love it inspired remains. That love can now flow into something else. When we love all things, we learn to let go and find peace even in impermanence."

Ravi nodded, a small smile breaking through his embarrassment. "I think I understand, Master."

Guided Meditation: The Garden of Love

The next morning, Ananda gathered his students in the monastery's lush garden. "Close your eyes," he instructed, his voice soft but commanding.

"Imagine yourself walking through this garden. Each flower represents someone or something you love. Notice their colors, their scents, their unique forms. Now, expand your gaze. See the flowers you've overlooked—the weeds, the thorns, the withered petals. Love them too, not for their perfection, but for their existence. Feel your heart growing, embracing all things equally.

Let this garden of love within you flourish."

The students' breaths slowed, their faces serene as they sat immersed in the imagery.

Love Without Borders

Over the weeks that followed, the students practiced expanding their love. Priya began tending to neglected corners of the garden. Arun, once impatient, listened more attentively during conversations. Ravi, who had been the most conflicted, began smiling at strangers, tending to animals, and cherishing even mundane tasks like sweeping the monastery floor.

One evening, Ravi approached Ananda beneath the banyan tree. "Master, I think I understand now. When we confine our love to one thing, we create fear, possessiveness, and conflict. But when we love freely and widely, we find peace."

Ananda's smile deepened. "Yes, Ravi. When love is expanded to all things, it ceases to be about possession and becomes a state of being. In that state, peace flows naturally."

Conclusion

Under the watchful gaze of the moon, the students sat in meditation, their hearts vast as the night sky. They had learned that love, when confined, could bring division and fear. But when expanded to encompass all things, it became a limitless source of peace. To love all things was to be at peace, and to be at peace was to truly live.

Affirmations

"My love is limitless, flowing freely to all beings and moments."

"As I expand my love, I release fear and embrace peace."

Questions for Reflection

1. What are the "single drops" in your life that you cling to? How might expanding your love bring balance?
2. Recall a time when loving one thing brought conflict or fear. How might expanding your perspective have changed the situation?
3. How can you practice loving something fleeting or imperfect today?

Dancing Buddha's Quote

"Love, when focused too narrowly, can bind and divide. But love, when shared freely, becomes peace itself."

STORY 17 – A LESSON IN NATURAL BALANCE

Introduction

The old monastery sat nestled at the edge of a sprawling forest, its stone walls humming with the whispers of the trees. Inside, Master Renshu, a kind and patient monk, guided his three students—Mei, Kento, and Hana—through life's mysteries. Each student came seeking peace, but today's lesson would come from an unexpected place: the small, everyday acts of eating and being.

"Master," Kento began one morning during their tea ceremony, "why is it so hard to resist foods that are bad for us?"

The monk smiled, the kind of smile that invited curiosity rather than answers. "Let us discover this together," he said. "Meet me by the hazelnut tree after the midday bell."

The students nodded, intrigued, unaware that their teacher had planned an adventure that would take them deep into the heart of their own cravings—and back to the natural rhythms of life.

The Lesson Begins

The three students gathered beneath the ancient hazelnut tree, its twisted branches heavy with nuts. Master Renshu waited with a wooden bowl filled with peanut butter and a small pile of fresh hazelnuts.

"Today, we will learn from the squirrels," he said, gesturing to a nearby branch where a furry-tailed creature nibbled contentedly.

Hana giggled. "The squirrels, Master?"

"Yes," Renshu said, his eyes twinkling. "Watch how they eat. They gather only what they need, and their food is simple. Yet they thrive in this forest."

He placed the bowl of peanut butter and a handful of hazelnuts before the students. "Now, imagine this peanut butter is a concentrated pleasure—like the foods many humans crave. Take a taste."

Each student dipped a finger into the rich, creamy peanut butter. Mei closed her eyes, savoring the intense flavor, while Kento licked his lips and reached for more.

"And now," Renshu said, handing them the fresh hazelnuts, "eat these as nature provides them."

The students cracked open the hazelnuts, tasting their subtle, earthy flavor. They were satisfying, but far less thrilling than the peanut butter.

"Which calls to you more strongly?" the monk asked.

"The peanut butter," Kento admitted. "It's sweeter, richer,

more exciting."

"Ah," Renshu said, "but is it natural? Does it belong in the forest?" He gestured to the squirrels. "You see, they do not crave peanut butter. They do not seek it, for it does not exist in their world. Nature has tuned them, just as it has tuned us, to desire what is good and balanced. But humans, with their cleverness, have created foods so concentrated that they disrupt this harmony."

He paused, his gaze softening. "A handful of ripe hazelnuts satisfies. It nourishes. But peanut butter, though made from nuts, has been altered, concentrated. It tricks the senses, making you desire more than you need. And so it is with all unnatural cravings—they create longing rather than satisfaction."

A Guided Meditation

Master Renshu led his students deeper into the forest, where a small clearing bathed in sunlight awaited. "Let us meditate here," he said, sitting cross-legged beneath a canopy of swaying branches.

"Close your eyes," he began, his voice soft and rhythmic, like the rustle of leaves in the breeze. "Imagine you are a squirrel, moving through this forest. You leap from branch to branch, the cool air brushing your fur. You feel hunger, not as a torment, but as a gentle signal guiding you."

The students breathed deeply, sinking into the imagery.

"You discover a hazelnut," Renshu continued. "Its shell is rough beneath your paws. You crack it open and taste its simple, earthy flavor. It satisfies you perfectly, no more and no less."

He paused, letting the silence settle like a soft blanket.

"Now, imagine you find a glass of sweet lemonade. It is

unnatural, overwhelming. You taste it, and it excites your senses in a way the nut never could. But it leaves you restless, longing for more. Your natural rhythm is disrupted."

As the students meditated, they felt the truth of the monk's words. The nut was enough; the lemonade was a storm.

"Repeat silently after me," Renshu said. "I honor my body's natural wisdom. I seek what nourishes me, not what excites me."

"Notice how your body already knows what feels natural and harmonious," he added. "Feel the clarity that comes when you align with nature."

When they opened their eyes, the world around them felt clearer, more vibrant.

Mei's Reflection

Later that evening, Mei approached Renshu by the fire pit. "Master, I've noticed that after meals, I crave sweets even when I'm not hungry. Why is that?"

Renshu smiled knowingly. "Ah, Mei, sometimes our cravings are not for food but for comfort. When you feel that craving, pause and ask yourself: What am I truly seeking? Often, it is not sweetness on the tongue but peace in the heart."

Mei nodded, her eyes reflecting both newfound understanding and a quiet determination to make changes.

The Fruit Flies

That evening, Renshu brought the students to the monastery kitchen. A glass of sweet lemonade sat on the counter, condensation beading on its surface. Fruit flies buzzed in a cloud above it.

"Observe," the monk said. "Even the smallest creatures are drawn to sweetness. But their attachment can trap them."

He carefully poured the lemonade down the drain and watched as the flies dispersed.

"Our cravings, like these flies, are natural but can become harmful when focused on what is unnatural. The lemonade is too much, too concentrated. But a ripe fruit, plucked from a tree, would guide them back to balance."

"Each craving is a message from within," he added, "inviting you to pause and explore what you truly need—whether it's nourishment, peace, or connection."

The Conclusion

One morning, beneath the hazelnut tree, Master Renshu addressed the students one last time. "Nature has gifted us the perfect nourishment—fruits, vegetables, nuts. They sustain us, connect us, and bring us into harmony with life. To embrace what is natural is to honor the body; to indulge in what is artificially concentrated is to invite imbalance. Remember, the body does not have an addiction problem—only the mind struggles with choice. And in every moment, the choice is yours: harmony or disruption."

As they reflected, Renshu added, "The path of harmony is not one of deprivation, but one of alignment with what truly nourishes the body and spirit."

The students bowed deeply, their hearts full of gratitude and understanding.

Affirmations

"I nourish my body with what is natural, embracing balance and harmony in all that I consume."

"I listen to my true needs, choosing what satisfies my soul rather than what merely excites my senses."

Questions for Further Reflection

1. What are some examples of natural foods or activities that bring you joy and balance?
2. When do you find yourself craving concentrated foods, and what emotions might be driving those cravings?
3. How can you incorporate the affirmation "I seek what nourishes me, not what excites me" into your daily life?
4. What steps can you take to return to a more natural and balanced way of eating and living?

Dancing Buddha's Quote

"To return to nature is to return to yourself. In simplicity, we find truth; in truth, we find peace."

STORY 18 – THE JAZZ OF COOPERATION

Introduction

The sun was setting over a small, bustling island in the Caribbean, where pastel-painted buildings leaned into narrow cobblestone streets. Life was vibrant yet tough; many of the islanders struggled to make ends meet, working long hours in the bustling markets, mending fishing nets by lantern light, or weaving baskets to sell to passing tourists. Amid the chaos, the humble monastery stood atop a hill, its wooden beams weathered by sea air and time.

The monk, a quiet man with an ever-present smile, sat on the steps of the monastery with his three students—Anya, Rohan, and Meera. In the warm evening air, the faint sound of jazz drifted from an old battery-powered radio propped on a windowsill nearby.

Marvin, the monastery's scrappy tomcat, lounged in the dirt, flicking his tail in time with the music. Around them, the hum of the island rose: laughter from a nearby food stall selling corndogs and the distant clatter of fishing boats returning home.

The monk looked at his students. "Today," he began, his voice as soothing as the ocean breeze, "we will learn the art of cooperation. It is like jazz: a melody that begins where harmony is easiest. Let me tell you a story."

Part 1: A Torn Dress and a Tomcat

The monk picked up Marvin and stroked his head, drawing the students' attention to the lazy cat.

"On this very island," he began, "there was a seamstress named Priya, known for her skill but constantly interrupted by Marvin, the mischievous tomcat. Marvin had a habit of sneaking into her shop, knocking over her canteen, and curling up on her fabrics, leaving them covered in fur.

"One day, Leena, a young woman from the village, stormed into Priya's shop with a torn dress in her hands. 'I need this fixed for tonight's celebration,' she said.

"As Priya examined the dress, Marvin pounced onto the counter, sending a basket of thread spools tumbling. Leena threw her hands in the air. 'How do you tolerate this cat? He's a menace!'

"Priya sighed. 'I've tried everything to keep him out, but he's too clever.'

"Leena huffed. 'Well, if you can't keep him out, I don't see how you can fix my dress.'

"At that moment, Marvin began batting at the torn edge of the dress, playing with the threads. Priya paused, watching him. She smiled. 'Maybe Marvin can help.'

"She tied a thread spool to a scrap of fabric and rolled it across the floor. Marvin chased it eagerly, his attention fully captured by the rolling thread. With him occupied, the workbench was clear, allowing Priya to focus on repairing the dress without further disruption. Marvin chased it eagerly, clearing the workbench of distractions. With her space free, Priya worked quickly and skillfully, repairing the dress.

"When she was done, Leena stared in amazement. 'You used the cat to help?'

"Priya laughed. 'I stopped fighting against him and started working with what he was ready to do. Cooperation doesn't always look how you expect.'

"Leena smiled for the first time that day. 'Perhaps I should try that with my neighbor. We've been fighting over where to hang the celebration lanterns. Maybe we can start with what we agree on.'"

Part 2: The Zipper of Cooperation

The students chuckled at the story. Anya was the first to speak. "So, Master, the lesson is to work with what's already there?"

The monk nodded. "Yes. Cooperation is like closing a zipper. You begin where the teeth are closest, where connection is easiest. Then, as you move upward, the rest follows naturally. Imagine two neighbors in a dispute over a shared fence. Instead of arguing about differences, they first agree on the need for privacy and safety. That shared understanding becomes the base, making it easier to resolve other details. Just like a zipper, cooperation begins with what is closest and builds upward.

"The mistake most people make is focusing on the widest

gap—the places where we are farthest apart. Those won't close until the base is secure."

Meera furrowed her brow. "But what if the gaps are too wide to close?"

The monk gestured toward the jazz playing on the radio. "Listen to this music. Do you hear how the musicians build on a single melody? They don't begin by playing wildly different notes. They start with harmony, with what they already agree on. Even the most divided people have some point of connection, no matter how small. Start there, and let the melody grow."

Rohan, skeptical as always, crossed his arms. "What if the other person doesn't want to cooperate?"

The monk smiled gently. "Then ask them a simple question: 'What are we ready to agree on?' Even a small 'yes' can open the door to greater harmony. When you establish these small agreements, you create momentum—like stepping stones leading toward deeper understanding."

Part 3: Guided Meditation: The Zipper Within

The monk stood and led the students to a clearing overlooking the ocean. The horizon was painted with hues of orange and pink, and the sound of waves crashing against the shore filled the air.

"Sit comfortably," the monk instructed. "As you close your eyes and take a deep breath, you may begin to notice the gentle rhythm of your breath, guiding you into a state of calm awareness."

His voice softened, matching the rhythm of the waves.

"Picture a torn dress, its edges frayed and disconnected. Now imagine a zipper lying beside it, waiting to bring the two sides together.

"Begin where the zipper teeth are closest. Feel the satisfaction of the first connection—the small click that signals unity. Notice how each step brings more alignment, how cooperation naturally unfolds, and how unity begins to take shape with ease. Slowly, the zipper moves upward, each click a point of agreement, a step toward wholeness.

"Now, imagine yourself as the torn dress. One side is your fear, doubt, and resistance. The other side is your hope, love, and willingness to connect. See the zipper moving upward, binding these parts of yourself into one.

"As the zipper closes fully, feel the smoothness of unity. You are whole. You are ready. Cooperation starts within, by uniting the pieces of yourself first."

The students' breathing slowed, their faces calm as they absorbed the imagery.

Affirmations

"I begin cooperation by finding our shared harmony."

"I build connection through small agreements that grow into unity."

Questions for Further Discussion

1. Think of a conflict in your life. What small point of agreement could you start with to build cooperation?
2. How can focusing on shared needs help you bridge divisions in relationships?

3. Reflect on a time when you successfully cooperated with someone. What allowed you to find common ground?
4. What can you learn from the metaphor of the zipper in your personal or professional relationships?

Conclusion

As the sky darkened and the first stars appeared, the students bowed to the monk. They lingered for a moment, watching Marvin bat playfully at a thread spool on the ground. The jazz continued to play softly, its melody weaving through the warm night air.

The monk gazed out at the ocean, his voice a whisper carried on the breeze. "Cooperation," he said, "is the art of beginning where we are closest, not where we are farthest apart. And as you reflect on this, you may find yourself wondering about the ways you've already begun to connect—perhaps even in ways you hadn't noticed before, much like a jazz melody that emerges from scattered notes, gradually forming a rhythm of understanding and unity."

And as the students walked back to the village, they carried the lesson with them, ready to find harmony in even the smallest connections.

Dancing Buddha's Quote:

"Cooperation is not found in forcing unity but in discovering harmony where it already exists. Begin with the notes that resonate, and the melody of understanding will follow."

Gregory K. Cadotte

STORY 19 – THE JOURNEY WITHIN

Introduction

In a remote mountain monastery surrounded by the snow-capped peaks of the Himalayas, Master Arun guided his students in the art of presence and compassion. The temple stood not far from a railway that wound its way through the valleys and climbed toward distant, bustling cities. The trains, often carrying tourists, merchants, and wanderers, were a rare connection to the outside world.

Master Arun's three students—Meera, a poet with a heart attuned to the unspoken; Jai, an adventurous spirit who loved capturing the world with his camera; and Leena, a quiet soul still learning to trust—each had their own struggles with staying present. Meera often found herself lost in thoughts of the past, Jai was constantly planning for the perfect shot in the future, and

Leena battled with fears that kept her from embracing the now.

One chilly morning, Master Arun announced, "We will take a train journey together. Pack lightly, for we will be carrying much more than our belongings."

They did not yet know that this journey would change them—but in ways even Master Arun could not have foreseen.

The students exchanged curious glances but said nothing, knowing that lessons with their teacher often unfolded like lotus petals—slowly, revealing beauty and wisdom. And as they considered this journey, perhaps they could already begin to wonder just how much they would discover.

Part 1: The Train and Chow-Baby

The students boarded the train with Master Arun, the rhythmic clatter of the wheels filling their ears as it began its ascent through the mountains. The train car was filled with a mix of travelers—families, solitary wanderers, and a few merchants clutching their goods.

Among them was a remarkable presence: Chow-Baby. Now three years old, Chow-Baby was known far and wide as a Buddha prodigy. His serene smile and unshakable calm had already become legendary. Despite his tender age, he practiced what many called "the living dharma," offering compassionate listening to soothe the emotionally wounded.

As Chow-Baby sat cross-legged on a seat, passengers approached him one by one. He listened intently, his tiny face glowing with understanding. A woman in tears left his side with a soft smile, as though her burdens had lightened. And as they spoke to him, they may have noticed something unexpected—perhaps a feeling of lightness, or a quiet shift within.

The students watched in awe. Meera whispered, "He's healing people with just his presence."

Master Arun nodded. "Chow-Baby understands something profound—that to truly listen is to offer love without condition. It is a skill we will all need on this journey."

Part 2: A Sudden Halt

As the train curved around a mountainside, it suddenly screeched to a halt. A landslide had blocked the tracks ahead. Passengers groaned, some pacing in frustration. Others argued with the conductor, their voices rising above the train's engine.

Jai raised his camera to capture the chaos, but Master Arun gently lowered it. "Not every moment is meant to be observed from a distance, Jai. Sometimes, we must step into the scene with compassion."

"But they're all so upset," Jai said. "What can we do?"

"Be present," Master Arun replied. "Pain seeks attention, not solutions. And as you listen, just notice how allowing space for another's experience can be enough."

Chow-Baby toddled over to a man muttering angrily about missed appointments. The child touched his hand, smiled, and said simply, "It's okay to feel sad."

The man's shoulders softened as though the weight he carried had been momentarily lifted. And as this shift happened, something deeper was taking place—perhaps a new way of seeing the world, a shift in perception, or a quiet recognition that emotions simply move like passing clouds.

Part 3: Compassionate Listening

As hours passed, the students practiced compassionate listening, just as Chow-Baby did. Meera sat beside a young woman who anxiously twisted a scarf in her hands. "I was supposed to meet my fiancé today," the woman said. "Now I don't know if I'll make it."

Meera didn't try to fix the problem or offer advice. Instead, she simply said, "That sounds really hard. I'm here with you."

Jai found himself sitting with a merchant fretting over his lost business. Instead of snapping another photo, Jai asked, "What would you like to share?" The man vented his worries, and Jai listened without judgment.

Leena, hesitant at first, joined a family struggling to keep their children calm. She sang a gentle song, and the children's tears turned to giggles.

Master Arun observed quietly, his face serene. "You are learning," he said. "When we stop chasing destinations—physical or emotional—we find we already have everything we need to offer love."

Part 4: Guided Meditation on Presence

As evening fell, the passengers grew quieter, the tension in the air dissolving into a shared stillness. Master Arun gathered the students and passengers in the train car for a meditation.

"Close your eyes now, and as you do, you may begin to notice the gentle stillness beneath you... and you may also realize that this stillness has always been there... like a mountain... steady, strong, and unwavering. Imagine your breath as a soft breeze, flowing in and out, bringing calm to every cell of your body."

The passengers inhaled and exhaled in unison.

"Now, picture the train surrounded by mountains, ancient and unmoving. These peaks have witnessed countless storms and still stand tall. They remind us that stillness is strength."

He paused, allowing the imagery to settle.

"Bring to mind someone here who seemed troubled. Imagine your heart as a glowing green light—the heart chakra. Let that light expand, wrapping them in love and understanding. And as you breathe, repeat these affirmations:

I am present in love and compassion.
I hold space for others to heal.
I breathe in peace and exhale love.
I am grounded in the moment.
My presence is a gift to the world."

When the meditation ended, the train car felt transformed. Passengers exchanged smiles, and even the once-angry voices were now softened.

Part 5: Moving On

At dawn, the tracks were cleared, and the train resumed its journey. As the mountains rolled past the windows, the students reflected on the experience.

Meera said, "I realized that being present is the greatest gift we can give."

Jai added, "I thought I needed my camera to capture moments, but today, I learned to capture them with my heart."

Leena, her voice quiet but sure, said, "I saw how holding space for others heals both them and myself."

Master Arun smiled. "You've each taken a step closer to understanding the living dharma. And as you take these lessons forward, you may notice how presence naturally deepens with practice."

Conclusion

When the students returned to the monastery, they carried with them not only memories of the journey but also a deeper understanding of the power of presence. And perhaps, in the days ahead, as they found themselves in moments of stillness, they may begin to notice... that the lessons of this journey are already a part of them, gently unfolding in ways they hadn't yet imagined. They had learned that physical movement does not guarantee emotional progress, and stillness does not equate to stagnation. By being present, they had discovered the art of loving and healing without conditions.

Questions for Further Discussion

1. What does Chow-Baby's ability to listen and heal teach us about presence and compassion?
2. How did the train's delay create an opportunity for growth and connection?
3. What does it mean to hold space for others emotionally? Can you think of a time when someone did this for you?
4. How can the affirmations "I am present in love and compassion" and "I hold space for others to heal"

help you in your daily life?
5. Why is it important to let go of attachment to destinations—whether physical or emotional?

Dancing Buddha's Quote

"Life's journey is not measured by how far we travel, but by how deeply we love in the stillness. Even when motionless, we can move mountains with compassion."

Gregory K. Cadotte

PART THREE

Letting Go

Gregory K. Cadotte

PART THREE

LETTING GO – FREEDOM THROUGH RELEASE

There is a profound paradox in life: the harder we hold on, the more elusive peace becomes. Clinging to the past, fearing inevitable changes, or resisting the natural flow of life creates an inner tension that binds the heart and clouds the mind. Letting go feels like a loss, but in truth, it is a liberation—a return to harmony. And when you begin to notice this... when you begin to feel this... you realize that letting go is not about losing—it is about freeing yourself to receive more than you ever imagined.

Imagine holding a handful of sand. Notice how, when you grip tightly, the grains slip through your fingers, scattering despite your efforts. But when your hand opens, the sand rests peacefully in your palm, held with ease. Just as the sand remains when you relax your grip, life's gifts stay with you when you stop trying to control what is beyond your grasp.

And you may find yourself wondering... what would happen if I softened my hold?

The Pain of Holding On

There was a time, perhaps not long ago, when you held on tightly. And that was okay. It felt necessary. It felt right. But notice now, as you reflect, the weight of what you have carried. Memories, relationships, old identities—things that once felt essential but now press upon your heart like heavy stones.

Take a moment to step back, as if watching from a distance. See yourself holding on, gripping tightly, and notice the strain in your hands, the tension in your shoulders. How does it feel? Now, imagine stepping just a little further back... just enough to observe... just enough to realize that you have the power to choose.

These emotions—grief, regret, and fear—are not enemies; they are messengers. They come to tell you that something is ready to be released. And as you listen to them, as you begin to truly hear their message, you might already feel a shift happening within you.

The Fear of Change

Fear speaks in whispers: *"What if letting go leads to emptiness? What if I lose control? What if the past, with all its pain, is still safer than the unknown?"*

It's okay to have these thoughts. Just for a moment, let them be there. Let them speak, but don't let them lead. Because, deep down, there is another voice—one that knows change is the most natural rhythm of all.

Consider the tree in autumn. The leaves do not fall in despair; they drift effortlessly, trusting in the promise of spring. The tree knows that releasing the old makes space for new growth. And you, like that tree, can let go—not with fear, but with trust. Because something new is waiting. Something lighter. Something freeing.

And as you think about this, you might already feel a new sensation—a sense of ease, a quiet knowing that everything is unfolding exactly as it should.

The stories and meditations in this section are designed to guide you through the process of release. They will invite you to explore the contrast between holding on and letting go—so you can truly feel the difference within yourself.

You will sit before *The Empty Chair*, where the weight of what is no longer there teaches the presence of love that never fades. You will grasp *The Ropes We Hold Onto* and discover that letting go is not about force, but about reaching for something better. And in *The Garden of Stillness*, you will come to see that you are not the ripples or reflections of life, but the vast and unshaken awareness beneath it all.

Each of these stories carries a gift—a realization, a shift in perspective. And as you move through them, at your own pace, in your own way, you may find that change is already unfolding within you.

The Healing Power of Letting Go

Letting go does not mean forgetting or abandoning. It means integrating. Honoring the past without being bound by it. You may find that, as you release attachment, a new sense of lightness emerges—one that was always there, just beneath the surface.

Picture yourself standing at the edge of a river, holding a stone. This stone represents what you are ready to release—a memory, a fear, a regret. Notice its weight in your hand. Feel its edges, its texture. Hold it for just a moment longer. Now, when you're ready, imagine casting it into the river. Watch it sink into the flowing water. Notice the ripples. And feel, in this moment, how much lighter you have become.

Because the river continues to flow. And so do you.

Meditations for Letting Go

These meditations are not just exercises; they are invitations. Invitations to step beyond old patterns, to rise above the currents of life, and to return to a state of deep, unshakable calm.

As you follow these guided experiences, you will:

Connect with your breath as an anchor, grounding you in the present.

Float above the weight of the past, soaring like a bird in an open sky.

Feel the healing light of acceptance, warming your heart and revealing that release is not an end—it is a beginning.

You can begin these meditations whenever you like. And as you do, you may notice that a sense of peace is already unfolding within you.

Affirmations for Release

Here are two affirmations to carry with you, spoken softly in the background of your thoughts, whispering change into being:

- *I release what no longer serves me, opening my heart to peace and renewal.*
- *I trust in the flow of life, knowing that each moment brings its own gifts.*

Moving Forward

As you step into this section, bring with you a sense of curiosity. Let these stories and meditations be an experience, a journey into yourself. Letting go is not a single act; it is a practice—a rhythm, a dance, a way of aligning yourself with the flow of life.

And as you move through this process, you may find something surprising: letting go is not about escaping—it is about coming home.

Because that peace you have been searching for? It has always been here, waiting for you to notice it.

Gregory K. Cadotte

STORY 20 - THE EMPTY CHAIR

Introduction: The Silent Bazaar

The sun hung low over a bustling marketplace in a small town in modern Pakistan. The streets were alive with the vibrant hum of daily life: merchants calling out prices, the rhythmic clatter of a mule pulling a cart laden with sacks of grain, and children darting between stalls, flying colorful kites that danced in the dusty breeze. Amid the noise, a kite snagged on the branches of a stick-like tree, its bright green tail fluttering helplessly against the bare wood.

The monk and his three students—Aadi, Leela, and Rohan—moved quietly through the crowd. They carried a simple wooden chair, its polished surface gleaming softly in the fading light.

"Master," Leela asked, struggling slightly with the chair's weight, "why do we bring this chair to such a crowded place? What lesson can it teach here?"

The monk gestured to the chaos around them. "The chair is a reminder," he said, his voice calm amid the noise. "Even in the busyness of life, it holds space for what is absent, for the love that remains unseen but ever-present. Today, we will learn to honor what we have lost."

They reached a quiet corner of the bazaar, where a lone candle flickered on a makeshift altar. The monk placed the chair beside it, the students gathering around him as the mule's cart creaked slowly past.

Section 1: The Weight of Loss

The chair stood empty against the backdrop of the bustling market, a stark contrast to the activity around it. The kite still hung tangled in the distant tree, its colors fading as the light dimmed.

"What do you see when you look at this chair?" the monk asked his students.

Leela tilted her head, her gaze fixed on the chair. "I see emptiness," she said. "It feels... lonely."

Rohan, his eyes on the candle beside the chair, added, "It reminds me of my grandfather. He used to sit in a chair like that while telling us stories. Now, when I think of him, it's as if the chair is all that's left."

The monk nodded. "Loss has a way of echoing in the spaces we once shared with those we love. This emptiness is not just absence—it is also a container for the love that remains."

Aadi, who had been silent, finally spoke. "But Master, if love remains, why does it hurt so much?"

"Because love stretches to hold what we have lost," the monk replied. "That stretch is what we feel as pain, but it is also what keeps our connection alive."

Section 2: The Kite and the Candle

The monk pointed toward the tree where the kite hung tangled. "Do you see that kite?"

The students nodded.

"It once soared freely, carried by the wind," the monk said. "Now it is caught, its movement stilled. But is it no longer a kite because it has been stopped?"

"No, Master," Leela replied. "It's still a kite, even if it's stuck."

"Exactly," the monk said. "Love, too, does not cease when its form changes. Like the kite, it may seem distant, but its essence remains."

He picked up the candle and placed it on the chair, the flame casting a warm glow over the empty space. "This flame represents the love we carry," he said. "It may flicker, but it does not go out. When someone we love is no longer with us, their light merges with our own, filling the emptiness with warmth."

Section 3: Guided Meditation: Honoring the Chair

The monk gestured for his students to sit in a circle around the chair. The faint sounds of the market hummed in the background, mingling with the soft rustle of the breeze.

"Close your eyes," the monk said, his voice steady and

soothing. "Let us honor what we have lost."

"Take a deep breath, feeling the earth beneath you. Let the noise of the market fade into the background, like waves retreating from the shore."

"Picture the empty chair before you. Let its presence invite you to remember someone or something you have lost."

"Now, imagine a soft light beginning to glow in the chair—a warm, golden flame, steady and calm. This light represents the love you shared, the moments you cherished."

"With each breath, let the light grow brighter, filling the space between you and the chair. Feel its warmth in your chest, a gentle reminder that love does not fade—it transforms."

"Silently repeat to yourself: 'What I have lost is not gone. It lives within me as love.' Let this truth settle into your heart like the steady glow of the candle."

The students breathed deeply, their faces softening as the meditation unfolded. The market sounds seemed distant now, their inner worlds quiet and expansive.

Section 4: The Love That Remains

When the meditation ended, the monk looked at each of his students. "Tell me," he said, "what did you feel?"

Aadi spoke first, his voice steady. "I thought of my mother. I've always focused on her absence, but in the meditation, I felt her love. It wasn't gone—it was within me."

Leela wiped a tear from her cheek. "I remembered my friend who passed away. I used to feel angry that she was taken so soon, but now... I see that the love we shared is still here."

Rohan nodded slowly. "The chair doesn't feel empty anymore, Master. It feels full—full of memories, of connection, of love."

The monk placed his hands together in gratitude. "Loss is never easy, my students, but it is not the end. The love we carry transcends time and space. When we honor what has been lost, we honor the love that remains, and in that love, we find presence."

Section 5: Carrying the Light

As they rose, the students noticed that the kite had slipped free from the tree. It floated gently to the ground, its journey paused but not over. The mule passed by again, its cart lighter now, the creak of its wheels almost melodic in the evening air.

The monk gestured to the chair. "Remember," he said, "the empty chair is not empty. It is filled with the light of love, which never fades. Like the kite freed from the tree, love transforms but remains whole."

The students carried the chair back through the market, their steps lighter and their hearts fuller.

Affirmations

"What I have lost is not gone. It lives within me as love."

"Love transforms absence into presence, and I carry it with me always."

Questions for Reflection

1. Who or what have you lost that still holds a place in your heart?
2. How can you honor the love you shared with them in your daily life?
3. What practices help you transform the pain of loss into the warmth of connection?

Dancing Buddha Quote

"The empty chair is not empty. It is filled with the love that endures, a light that never fades."

The Empty Chair teaches us that while loss brings pain, it also reveals the enduring power of love. By honoring what has been lost and embracing the love that remains, we find connection and presence even in absence. Through this understanding, we transform grief into gratitude and emptiness into light.

STORY 21 - THE ROPES WE HOLD

Introduction

In a quiet monastery nestled in the misty hills of Tibet, a warm fire crackled in the hearth of the main hall. It was autumn, and the earthy scent of roasted butternut squash wafted through the air from the kitchen, mingling with the subtle fragrance of aged parchment and incense. The flickering candlelight cast gentle shadows along the wooden beams, lending the room an air of quiet reverence.

Two students, Sora and Leila, sat cross-legged on cushions, waiting for their teacher, Master Han, to begin the evening's lesson. The anticipation in the air was thick, though neither of them spoke. Their young minds were eager, their hearts open yet burdened by unspoken questions.

By their side was Marvy, a junior monk visiting from a neighboring monastery. Marvy was earnest but young, his sharp curiosity often teetering on impatience. At his feet lay Willy Two Shoes, a tiny, mischievous wiener dog with an uncanny ability to match his owner's restless energy. Willy gnawed on a frayed rope toy, tugging and twisting with determined enthusiasm.

As Master Han entered the room, his calm presence seemed to settle the flickering of the flames. He carried a wooden bowl of roasted butternut squash, setting it down beside him before taking his seat. He gazed at his students, his eyes reflecting the wisdom of many seasons.

"Tonight," he began, his voice resonant and steady, "we will speak of the ropes we hold. And as you listen, you might begin to wonder... what would it feel like to let go effortlessly, only when the time feels right?"

Part 1: The Ropes of Security

Master Han gestured toward Willy Two Shoes, who was engaged in an intense battle with his rope toy, growling in playful defiance as he refused to relinquish it.

"See how Willy clings to his rope?" Master Han observed. "To him, it is not merely a toy—it is security. Even though it is worn and ragged, he will not let it go unless he has another to grab onto."

Leila frowned, watching the little dog's stubborn grip. "But Master, what if the rope is harmful? Shouldn't we force ourselves to let it go?"

Master Han shook his head gently, his expression kind. "No,

Leila. Pressure creates resistance. Even when we recognize a habit or belief as unhealthy, we often hold onto it because it feels safe. If we force ourselves to let go, fear grips us even tighter. Instead, we must offer ourselves a new rope—something stronger, healthier, and more secure. Only then will we release the old one willingly."

Marvy leaned forward, his brow furrowed. "But isn't it better to let go quickly? To move on without clinging to the past?"

Master Han smiled. "Patience, Marvy. Even the strongest climbers do not release one hand until they have a firm grip on another hold. Let me tell you a story... There was once a traveler who wandered through a dense forest, clinging to an old walking stick. One day, he found a stronger, sturdier staff, but he hesitated. 'What if this one is not as reliable?' he thought. But as he walked, he began using the new staff more and more, until one day, he realized he had left the old one behind without even noticing. Life is no different. Let the process unfold naturally. Add new, healthier ropes until the old ones fall away."

Part 2: Yahweh Drops In

At that moment, the air in the room seemed to shift. A presence, vast and unexplainable, filled the space, pressing gently against the edges of reality. A deep, resonant voice echoed from nowhere and everywhere.

"Master Han," the voice intoned, "you speak of patience, of ropes and security. Do you not know that I, Yahweh, once demanded people let go of all things at once?"

The students gasped, their eyes widening. Willy Two Shoes barked furiously, his tiny body vibrating with excitement.

Master Han bowed his head in reverence. "Welcome,

Yahweh. Indeed, you asked for complete surrender. And your power moved mountains, inspired faith. But not all are ready for such surrender at once. For many, the process must be gentle, gradual. The human heart clings tightly to what it knows."

The presence softened, the voice quieter now. "And what do you offer them, then, if not command?"

Master Han gestured to the bowl of butternut squash. "I offer them this: nourishment, warmth, and new possibilities. I offer them new ropes to hold onto until they are ready to let go. And often, as they find something new to grasp, they realize the old was never holding them—it was only their own hands that refused to let go."

The presence lingered for a moment, then seemed to smile—a feeling more than a sight. "Very well, Master Han. Let us see how you guide them."

Part 3: The Ropes We Hold

Master Han turned back to his students. He picked up the frayed rope toy and held it alongside a fresh, sturdy rope.

"Imagine this old rope as a habit that no longer serves you. Perhaps it is a fear, an addiction, or a belief that limits your growth. You cling to it because it feels safe, even as it frays and weakens. Now imagine this new rope as a healthier choice—an act of kindness, a moment of mindfulness, a nourishing thought.

"You do not need to let go of the old rope immediately. Simply begin to hold the new one alongside it. Over time, you will find yourself reaching for the new rope more often, until one day, the old one falls away without pressure or force."

Sora raised a hand. "But what if we don't know what the new rope should be? What if we're afraid to grab it?"

Master Han placed the new rope in Sora's hand. "Fear is natural, but it fades with familiarity. Begin with small steps. If your habit is self-criticism, your new rope could be a single act of self-kindness. If your habit is avoidance, your new rope could be one small act of courage. Each small step strengthens the new rope until it feels like home."

Part 4: Guided Meditation: The Ropes of Life

Master Han guided the students to close their eyes. Willy Two Shoes curled up on Marvy's lap, finally still.

"Take a deep breath," Master Han said, his voice slow and soothing, "and as you exhale, just notice... how your body begins to settle, how your mind begins to open. And as you listen, you may find yourself drifting... as if something inside is beginning to understand, even before your conscious mind does."

"Picture yourself standing in a great canyon. The walls rise high around you, and a sturdy rope hangs from above. This rope is your lifeline, your habit, your comfort.

"Now, see that this rope is fraying. It is no longer strong, yet you cling to it because it feels safe.

"Above you, another rope begins to lower. It is thick, strong, and vibrant with color. This rope feels unfamiliar, but as you touch it, you feel its strength.

"Hold both ropes. There is no need to let go of the old one yet. Simply feel the new rope, its steadiness, its promise. And as you hold it, you might begin to notice... how natural it is to trust what feels right. Perhaps, without even trying, you'll find yourself reaching for it more and more." Over time, you will begin to trust it more. And one day, without even realizing it, you will release the old rope and climb higher with the new."

Affirmations

"I allow myself to hold both the old and the new as I grow into healthier habits."

"I trust the process of gentle change and let go when the time is right."

"With each small step, I strengthen my new path and embrace my growth."

Questions for Further Discussion

1. What old ropes—habits or beliefs—are you holding onto, and why?
2. What new ropes can you introduce into your life to create positive change?
3. How can you practice patience with yourself during periods of growth?
4. What does the presence of no-pressure change mean to you?

Conclusion

As the fire crackled softly and the scent of roasted squash lingered, Master Han watched his students rise and bow. Yahweh's presence had faded, but his essence remained, a reminder of the balance between surrender and gentle guidance.

"Remember," Master Han said, his voice gentle, "the ropes

you hold have simply been part of your journey. And as you grow, you might begin to wonder… will you notice the shift now, or later, as the change unfolds in its own way?" They are tools for your journey. No pressure is required; only the willingness to reach for something better."

The students bowed deeply, their hearts lighter, their minds clearer. As they stepped into the cool night air, the wiener dog trotted after them, tugging his frayed rope toy with joy. Above them, the stars seemed to shine brighter, like new ropes waiting to be grasped.

Dancing Buddha's Quote

"You do not have to drop the past to reach for the future—simply hold both, and in time, one will let go of you."

Gregory K. Cadotte

STORY 22 – THE GARDEN AND THE FLOWER

Introduction

In a tranquil valley, surrounded by rolling hills and blossoming trees, there lay a monastery known as the Garden of Stillness. Its heart was a serene garden filled with vibrant flowers, a glistening pool, and ancient stone pathways that led to moments of profound insight. Here, a monk named Master Ananda guided his students on the path to self-discovery. Among them were three students: Maya, whose mind was a tempest of thoughts; Kiran, who wrestled with insecurities of the body; and Ravi, who sought to understand his place in the universe.

This is the story of how they learned the profound truth that we are not our thoughts, nor our bodies, but the conscious space where forms arise and dissolve.

The Invitation to the Pool

One morning, Master Ananda called his students to the edge of the glistening pool in the garden. The water shimmered like liquid sunlight, reflecting the vibrant flowers and the azure sky.

"Today," Master Ananda began, his voice soft yet resonant, "we will explore the nature of who we truly are. Let us begin with a simple observation. Look at the pool. What do you see?"

Maya leaned forward. "I see the reflection of the trees, the flowers, and the sky."

Kiran added, "I see my own reflection."

Ravi hesitated. "I see the ripples, distorting everything."

Master Ananda smiled. "Each of you sees something unique, yet the pool remains unchanged. Thoughts are like the ripples, bodies like the reflections, but what holds them all?" He paused, letting the question hang in the air. "Come, let us explore deeper."

The Lesson of the Garden

Walking through the garden, Master Ananda led them to a tree heavy with blossoms.

"Maya," he said, "close your eyes and imagine a storm. The wind howls, the rain lashes. What do you feel?"

Maya's breath quickened. "I feel chaos and fear."

"Now," he continued, "imagine the storm passing. The sun shines, and the garden blooms again. What do you feel?"

Maya's lips curved into a smile. "Peace."

"Notice," Master Ananda said, "how your feelings shifted, yet the garden, like your true self, remained constant beneath it all. You are not the storm, nor the sun—you are the garden, holding all experiences."

Turning to Kiran, Master Ananda gestured toward the glistening pool. "Kiran, what do you notice about your reflection in the water?"

"It changes as I move," Kiran replied.

"Exactly," said the monk. "Your body, like your reflection, is ever-changing, yet the pool remains. You are not the reflection, but the clear water beneath. Feel this clarity, like the stillness within you that holds every movement."

Finally, Master Ananda faced Ravi. "Do you see how the flowers grow here, in harmony? Each has its place, yet none claims ownership of the garden. What does this teach you?"

Ravi pondered. "That I am part of something greater... a gardener tending to forms but not bound by them."

Master Ananda nodded. "Exactly. And as the gardener, you hold the space for all growth. Tend it with care, but do not mistake the garden for yourself."

Guided Meditation by the Pool

The four sat by the pool as a soft breeze carried the scent of jasmine. Master Ananda's voice guided them into a state of stillness.

"Close your eyes and take a deep breath. Feel the coolness of the air entering your lungs, anchoring calmness within you. Imagine the pool before you, its surface calm and clear. With each breath, let go of the ripples of thought, allowing the water to become still."

Maya's shoulders relaxed. Kiran's restless fingers grew still. Ravi's furrowed brow softened.

"Now," Master Ananda continued, "see the flowers in the

garden, each unique, each beautiful, yet none grasping to be more than it is. Feel your body as part of this garden, ever-changing yet perfect in its unfolding.

"Finally, become the space itself—the air, the light, the conscious potential where the garden blooms. You are not the forms within the space; you are the infinite canvas holding them all."

His voice softened further, a rhythmic cadence: "And as you settle into this stillness, you may notice a growing sense of peace, as though the vastness of your true self is gently expanding."

As his voice faded, the students remained in stillness, each immersed in the vastness within.

The Lesson Deepens

After the meditation, Master Ananda asked each of them to share what they experienced.

Maya spoke first. "When I let go of the ripples, I felt a stillness I didn't know was there. It was as if the chaos in my mind was never truly me."

Master Ananda nodded. "That stillness is always within you, Maya. It is the garden that holds the storm and the sun, yet remains untouched by either."

Kiran said, "I realized my body is like a reflection in the water, always changing but never defining what I truly am."

"Yes," Master Ananda affirmed. "Your body is a beautiful part of the garden, but not its essence. Learn to appreciate its role without mistaking it for the whole. And as you reflect on this, notice how naturally this understanding brings ease."

Ravi was quiet for a moment before speaking. "I felt like I was everything and nothing at the same time. The flowers, the water, the light... they're all connected, and yet none of them are the gardener."

Master Ananda smiled. "Exactly, Ravi. When you see yourself as both the gardener and the garden, you understand the interplay of form and formlessness. Tend the forms, but know you are the space that allows them to grow. And in this understanding, there is profound freedom."

Affirmations

Before leaving, Master Ananda shared two affirmations:

"I am not my thoughts; I am the stillness in which they arise and dissolve."

"I am not my body; I am the infinite space where all forms emerge and return."

He encouraged the students to carry these truths in their hearts, repeating them daily to nurture their awareness. "And with each repetition, you may find these truths blooming effortlessly within you."

Conclusion

In the days that followed, Maya found herself less entangled in the storms of her mind. She began to watch her thoughts as clouds passing through the sky of her awareness. Kiran started to appreciate his body as a reflection—changing yet beautiful in its impermanence. Ravi embraced his role as a simple gardener, tending the forms of life without attachment.

One evening, as the sun set over the hills, Master Ananda gathered them once more by the pool.

"Remember," he said, "you are not the ripples nor the reflections. You are the conscious space where all arises and dissolves. Tend your garden with care, but do not mistake the forms for the gardener."

The students bowed in gratitude, their hearts lighter, their minds clearer.

Questions for Reflection

1. How do your thoughts and emotions shape your experience of the present moment?
2. In what ways can you create space between your identity and the ever-changing nature of your body?
3. What practices can help you connect with the stillness within?

Dancing Buddha's Quote

"The gardener does not become the flower, nor the earth, nor the sun. The gardener simply tends the garden, knowing it is not separate from the whole."

STORY 23 – THE SILENT TEACHER

Part 1: The Question

In a small monastery nestled high in the mountains, the air was crisp and the sounds of the world seemed muted by the vast expanse of nature. A young student named Arun approached his teacher, Master Dev, with a question that had been troubling him.

"Master," Arun began, his tone hesitant but earnest, "there are so many teachers, so many teachings. How do I know which teacher to listen to? Whose path should I follow?"

Master Dev, seated cross-legged on a simple mat, looked up from his cup of tea. His face bore the calmness of one who had weathered countless storms. He gestured for Arun to sit beside him.

"Listen to all teachers, Arun," the monk said, his voice gentle. "Every teacher—whether they speak in words or actions—has something to teach. But do not mistake listening for following. You must follow what resonates with your path at this moment.

In doing so, you will find that you are not taught by any one teacher but by all. You will become self-taught through their lessons."

Arun frowned slightly. "But Master, how do I know which lessons are right for me?"

Master Dev smiled knowingly. "Ah, that is the challenge, isn't it? Most teachers are teachers of discontentment. They teach a version of contentment too small to encompass all things. These teachers are so discontent themselves that they've built their own ideas of how the world should be and try to pass these ideas to others. They teach you to grasp for fleeting things, to seek happiness outside yourself. But the true teacher, Arun, is the one who teaches contentment—not through words, not through concepts, but through presence and acceptance."

The student leaned forward, curiosity sparking in his eyes. "How do I find this teacher of contentment?"

Master Dev sipped his tea thoughtfully. "Look within, Arun. In your meditation, in your studies, seek out the one who does not clamor for attention, who does not demand or plead. This teacher of contentment is waiting, but you must be patient. Sit with yourself and listen."

Arun nodded, determination lighting his face. He bowed to his teacher and left the room, resolved to find this mysterious teacher of contentment.

Part 2: The Search

For the next week, Arun meditated diligently. He sat under the ancient pine tree in the monastery courtyard, listening to the wind whisper through its branches. He studied the sacred texts with fervor, hoping their wisdom would lead him to the teacher.

Yet, despite his efforts, he found no trace of the teacher of contentment. Instead, his mind seemed louder than ever—his thoughts a cacophony of doubts, regrets, and longings.

By the week's end, frustration boiled over. Arun stormed back to Master Dev, his face flushed with exasperation. His mind churned with self-doubt and impatience, replaying his efforts over and over—each meditation session, each text studied, each silent moment under the pine tree. The more he tried, the farther away the answer seemed to be. It felt as though he was failing not just himself, but his teacher.

"Master!" he exclaimed. "I have done everything you said. I meditated, I studied, I searched within myself. But I cannot find this teacher of contentment you speak of. It's as if it doesn't exist!"

Master Dev chuckled, his laughter a warm, resonant sound that filled the room. Arun stared at him, baffled.

"What's so funny, Master?" Arun asked, his tone edged with impatience.

The monk wiped his eyes, still smiling. "Arun, my dear student, I forgot to tell you something about this teacher of contentment. It is so content that it is silent. It does not need to call out to you, does not need to convince you of its presence. It moves at the speed of reality itself, so fully accepting that it never feels the need to speak. It waits patiently for you to notice it, for it is never so uncomfortable that it must announce itself."

Arun blinked, his frustration giving way to intrigue. "Silent? Then... how am I supposed to learn from it?"

Master Dev gestured to the mat beside him. "Sit, Arun. Sit with this teacher of contentment. Ask it how it can remain so at peace in a world filled with emotional pain. And listen, not with your ears, but with your heart."

Part 3: The Discovery

That evening, Arun returned to the courtyard. He sat beneath the pine tree, the evening breeze cool against his skin. Closing his eyes, he quieted his mind as best he could. He waited for the teacher of contentment to appear, though no voice spoke, no vision arose. Still, he remained, allowing the stillness to envelop him.

As the minutes stretched into hours, something began to shift. Arun felt an unexpected sense of ease creeping into his chest, a quiet warmth that didn't come from the world around him but from within. It was as though a presence had emerged—not in words, but in being.

With his eyes still closed, Arun posed his question silently: *Teacher of contentment, how can you remain so deeply at peace in a world filled with both joy and suffering?*

The answer came not in language but in a deep, undeniable knowing, as if the response arose from the very core of his being:

I am at peace because I do not resist and have the knowledge that allows me to do so easily. Pain and joy are threads in the fabric of existence and they flow to teach you something. Emotional pain arises when we narrow our view and resist the flow of life. But when we reflect the openness of reality, pain dissolves into understanding, leaving space for harmony to emerge. I do not hold onto pain, nor do I flee from it. Instead, I transform it and let it pass through, like a river carving its path through a vast valley, shaping the land as it flows. All experiences, even suffering, have their place in the greater whole – and that place is to teach you. To resist them is to create discontentment. To learn from them, to align with the fullness of reality's teachings is to transcend pain and discover the infinite peace that already exists within.

Part 4: A Guided Meditation

Arun felt his breath deepen, his shoulders relax. The presence continued:

I do not fight reality, for reality is not my enemy. Suffering is not created by the world; it arises from the resistance we bring to it. When you can sit with your pain, not as something to battle or escape, but as a part of life to witness, you will find that it begins to soften. Pain exists to teach and remind you of what matters, of what you hold dear. It is not your adversary, but your guide, pointing you toward truth and growth.

Take a moment to close your eyes. Imagine yourself sitting under a great, ancient tree. Feel the ground beneath you, steady and unyielding, supporting you completely. Notice your breath, flowing naturally, as constant as the river of life. Allow any discomfort or pain to surface, not as something to avoid, but as part of the landscape of your experience. See it as a cloud drifting across a vast sky—temporary, ever-changing, and unable to obscure the infinite openness above. Breathe deeply, and with each breath, let go of resistance. Embrace the peace that emerges when you allow life to simply be.

Part 5: The Lesson

Arun's eyes widened, and a single tear slid down his cheek—not from sadness, but from a deep sense of release. He realized how much energy he had wasted battling his emotions, labeling them as good or bad, clinging to joy, and rejecting sorrow. Yet here, in the presence of this silent teacher, he saw the truth: contentment wasn't the absence of pain, but the acceptance of it—the willingness to let discomfort expand his heart and mind until pain transformed into understanding.

At that moment, Arun repeated an affirmation softly, allowing it to root deeply within him:

I embrace all experiences with peace, knowing that each one is a step on my path.

The weight of his previous struggles began to lift, replaced with an unwavering acceptance of life as it unfolded. He sat with the teacher of contentment for what felt like hours, feeling more grounded with each breath.

When Arun opened his eyes, the night sky stretched above him, stars twinkling in the vast expanse. The world felt different—gentler, more alive. He bowed his head, a silent gesture of gratitude to the teacher of contentment that had spoken without words.

Affirmations

"I embrace all of life's experiences with openness, knowing that peace is found in acceptance, not resistance."

"I release the need to fight or flee from emotions; instead, I allow them to flow through me, transforming into wisdom and understanding."

Questions for Further Discussion

1. How can we learn to embrace both joy and pain as part of life's experiences?
2. What practices help us connect with our inner "teacher of contentment"?

3. How does resisting emotions differ from accepting them? What impact does this have on our peace of mind?

Dancing Buddha's Quote

"Silence is the language of peace. In stillness, all answers arise."

Gregory K. Cadotte

STORY 24 – THE DANCE OF IMPATIENCE

Introduction

The evening sun dipped low, casting a warm amber glow over the valley road that wound like a ribbon through the forest. The air carried a faint scent of pine, mingled with the earthy aroma of fallen leaves, and the distant chirping of birds added a gentle melody to the scene. In the passenger seat of a modest, weathered car, a young student sat with his arms folded, his jaw tight, fingers drumming against the armrest. His knee bounced restlessly. Each red light ahead felt like a barrier between him and where he wanted to be.

The monk, his master, sat behind the wheel, humming a tune as his hands rested lightly on the steering wheel, unbothered by the slow pace.

"This is unbearable," the student muttered, shifting in his seat. The cars ahead inched forward, and the brake lights of the vehicle in front pulsed like a heartbeat, rhythmic and steady. "We'll be late at this rate. Why don't we take a different route or try to overtake these cars?"

The monk glanced at the student, his expression calm, like a pond untouched by the wind. "Late for what?" he asked softly.

"For…well, for everything!" The student gestured at the road. "The day is passing us by, and we're stuck here. Isn't it natural to want to get moving?"

The monk smiled, his hands steady as the car crept forward. "Natural, yes. But is it helpful? Impatience, you see, often blinds us to the lessons in the moment and ties our peace to an uncertain future. And the more we resist where we are, the more we create struggle inside ourselves. Is that a helpful path?"

The student frowned, his breath shallow. He could still feel the pressure in his chest, the restless need to be elsewhere.

The Dance of Impatience

"Let me show you something," the monk said. He eased the car into the left lane, overtaking a vehicle, then another, weaving deftly through the traffic. For a brief moment, they gained ground. The student felt a flicker of satisfaction—until they reached a bottleneck and were forced to stop entirely.

"See?" the student said, slumping back into his seat. "Now we're stuck again."

The monk chuckled, returning to the original lane. "That is the dance of impatience," he said. "You gain a little here, lose a little there, but the underlying feeling remains unchanged."

The student raised an eyebrow. "What feeling?"

"Impatience is a focus too tightly fixed on the self," the monk said. "It arises when we see only our own path, our own desires, and measure the world by how quickly it aligns with them. But if we take a step back, if we soften our gaze, we might begin to see a larger pattern, a rhythm beneath it all."

The student sighed. "But it *feels* like we should be moving faster."

"Only because your mind has decided this moment is a problem," the monk said. "What if this moment was exactly as it should be?"

The Pace of Reality – Many Journeys at Once

The cars inched forward again. "But isn't it natural to want to get where you're going?" the student asked.

"Of course," the monk said. "But impatience distorts that natural desire. It tricks us into thinking that our happiness depends on the future, on arriving somewhere. It binds us to a place that does not yet exist, making the present feel like an obstacle instead of an experience."

The student exhaled sharply. "Then what should we focus on instead? The cars in front of us? The red lights?"

The monk shook his head and gestured out the window. "Look there."

The student followed his gaze. Along the side of the road, a family of deer grazed in the golden light. Their movements were slow, deliberate, each step placed with care. A fawn lifted its head, its ears twitching as it looked directly at the car.

"They're not in a hurry," the monk said. "Their pace is the pace of reality—steady, unhurried, in tune with their surroundings. Now look at the people in these cars." He waved at the line of vehicles around them.

The student glanced around. In one car, a driver pounded his steering wheel, his face red with frustration. In another, a woman furiously tapped at her phone, her jaw tight. The student felt a pang of recognition. He had *been* these people, clenched in frustration, believing he was stuck.

"They all seem…angry," he said.

"Or anxious, or sad," the monk said. "But what if I told you that we are always on many journeys at once? There is the journey of the body—the miles we travel, the places we wish to reach. But there is also the journey of the heart—the way we move through love, kindness, and connection. And the journey of the spirit—the deepening of our awareness, our understanding, our ability to simply *be*."

The student listened, his breath slowing.

"When traffic halts, only the physical journey is paused. But the others? The journey of love continues when you send good thoughts to the driver beside you. The journey of awareness expands when you notice the golden light on the treetops instead of the brake lights ahead. The journey of being present deepens every time you breathe and realize *this* moment is not empty—it is alive."

The student swallowed. "So, even now, I am still moving?"

The monk nodded. "In every way that truly matters."

A Guided Meditation

The student nodded slowly, though his fingers still drummed against the armrest. "But what can we do when the moment feels unbearable, like this traffic? It's like my chest is tightening, and my mind keeps telling me we're wasting time."

The monk smiled and pulled the car to a stop as the vehicles ahead paused again. "Close your eyes for a moment," he instructed. "Let's try something."

The student hesitated but obeyed, settling into his seat.

"Take a deep breath," the monk said. "Inhale slowly through your nose… and exhale gently through your mouth. Feel the cool air entering your nostrils, filling your lungs, and expanding your chest. As you exhale, notice the warmth of the breath leaving your body, carrying tension away."

The student's breathing began to slow.

"Now," the monk continued, "picture yourself as a river. The water flows naturally, moving around rocks and bends without resistance. Imagine your thoughts and frustrations as leaves floating on the surface. Watch them drift away, carried by the current. There is no need to hold onto them."

A sense of calm began to settle over the student.

"Now bring your awareness to the present," the monk said. "Feel the seat beneath you, the sound of the engine, the light filtering through the trees. This moment is whole, complete. And within this stillness, you are not waiting. You are *traveling inward*, deepening into presence, love, and peace."

The student exhaled deeply, his shoulders relaxing. "It feels…lighter," he said softly.

And for the first time that evening, he *meant* it.

Moving Forward

As they crested a hill, the sun dipped below the horizon, painting the sky in hues of violet and gold. The student gazed out the window, watching the deer fade into the forest. "I think I understand," he said. "No journey ever really stops."

The monk smiled. "Exactly. Every moment offers movement—if we know where to look."

And so they drove on, moving at the pace of reality, one moment at a time, grounded in the truth that they were exactly where they needed to be.

Affirmations

I am where I need to be—physically, emotionally, and spiritually. Every moment offers a new journey.

I trust the flow of life. Whether moving or still, I am always growing, always becoming.

Questions for Further Discussion

1. How can impatience distort your perception of the present moment, and how does shifting focus change your experience?
2. What techniques help you reconnect with the present when you feel overwhelmed?
3. In what ways are you always moving forward, even when life appears to be at a standstill?
4. How can you cultivate deeper awareness of your emotional and spiritual journeys during moments of physical stillness?
5. What does it mean to move at the pace of reality? How does this apply to your daily life?

Dancing Buddha's Quote

"Patience is not the art of waiting but the wisdom of moving with life's rhythm—step by step, breath by breath, journey by journey."

Gregory K. Cadotte

STORY 25 – THE ANGEL IN THE TEMPLE

Introduction

In the heart of New York City, amidst the hum of honking taxis, bustling sidewalks, and towering skyscrapers, there stood an old brick building sandwiched between two apartment complexes. It was a quiet refuge in the chaos of the inner city, known simply as "The Center." Inside, a monk named Kavi had transformed an unused community hall into a space for reflection and learning.

Kavi sat on a worn cushion near a cracked window that let in the faint sound of distant sirens and the aroma of spiced chai from a nearby café. His two students, Arun and Leela, sat cross-legged on the wooden floor, their expressions curious but weary from the pace of city life.

On a nearby table, Kavi had placed a bowl of ripe dates, a brass singing bowl, and a steaming pot of herbal tea—seemingly random items but carefully chosen for the day's lesson.

"Today," Kavi began, his voice calm amidst the noise outside, "as you begin to explore the angel within your body-temple, you may notice a growing awareness of its presence—your consciousness. And we'll learn how to protect it from the traps of the world around us."

Part 1: The Wizard and the Eternal Now

Kavi picked up the singing bowl and rang it gently, letting its resonant tone fill the space.

"Once," he began, "there was a wizard who wandered the world, guiding lost souls. He carried a peculiar watch—one without hands—and told those he met, 'This watch shows the only time that matters: the Eternal Now.'

"One day, the wizard walked through a city much like this one, where angels descended to guide humanity with their light. But along the streets, establishments designed to ensnare visitors were everywhere—bright neon signs, alluring scents of food carts, and shops offering endless pleasures.

"The angels, curious about human sensations, stopped to explore. They tasted, touched, and experienced, each new pleasure pulling them deeper into the city. Soon, they forgot their mission, distracted by their newfound habits.

"The wizard tried to call them back, holding up his watch as a reminder of the Eternal Now. But they were too entranced by the noise and the lights. Their love for these sensations had trapped them, not out of malice but because they felt so good in their human forms."

Part 2: Conscious Love and the Body-Temple

Kavi set the singing bowl down and gestured to the bowl of dates on the table.

"Our consciousness," he said, "is like those angels—pure, radiant, and full of love. It resides in the body-temple, our vessel for this journey. But our most powerful essence—our ability to love—is also what makes us vulnerable. Love follows where we lead it, without judgment. And if we are not mindful, this loving consciousness can become ensnared by the physical body, which has been shaped for millions of years by simpler instincts: survival, pleasure, repetition."

He picked up a date and held it delicately. "Imagine your consciousness entering a market stall filled with fragrant, ripe dates. The sweetness is irresistible. You stay, savoring each bite, enjoying the moment. But what happens if you never leave? The stall becomes your world, and the journey you began fades from memory."

Leela frowned. "Master, are you saying that love can trap us?"

Kavi nodded gently. "Love is the most powerful force, but it is also unquestioning. Your consciousness loves you so much that it follows wherever you lead. If you indulge in habits that feel good but weaken your body-temple—overeating, overindulging, or chasing fleeting pleasures—your consciousness does not resist. It merges with the experience, believing it is serving you.

"That is why we must be mindful of what we allow into our temple. Our instincts were built for a simpler time, when the body needed to seek out food and pleasure for survival. But now, surrounded by abundance and stimulation, those same instincts can lead us astray. Habits that once served us can become chains, binding the angel within."

Kavi's expression softened as he continued, "And because love is at the core of our being, it magnifies whatever it becomes attached to. In its natural state, love flows freely, connecting, expanding, lifting. But when concentrated inputs—overstimulating foods, addictive technologies, endless entertainment—flood the body-temple, love, too, concentrates unnaturally. It transforms into attachment, binding itself to that which excites it most."

Arun sat forward. "So love can become addiction?"

Kavi nodded. "Yes, in a way. When love, meant to be infinite and expansive, is funneled into something artificial—something too intense, too fast, too stimulating—it loses its freedom. Instead of lifting us higher, it pulls us into fixation. The body, shaped over millions of years for much simpler inputs, is overwhelmed. And because love moves with us unconditionally, it clings to whatever we give it, even if it leads us away from peace."

Part 3: Tea and the Flow of Consciousness

Kavi poured steaming tea into three small cups, the fragrant steam curling into the air like wisps of thought.

"Tea flows freely," he said, "but if you pour it into a cup and never drink, it grows cold, its essence lost. Our consciousness is like this tea—it is meant to flow, to evolve, to adapt. But when it becomes too attached to the body's old programming—cravings, fears, urges—it stagnates, like a forgotten cup left to cool."

Arun sipped his tea thoughtfully. "So, Master, how do we avoid these traps? How do we keep our consciousness free?"

Kavi's eyes gleamed with wisdom. "By becoming gatekeepers of our body-temple, and as you take on this role, you may find yourself naturally making choices that nourish you. Before bringing anything inside—whether it's food, drink, thoughts, or experiences—ask yourself: Will this nourish the angel within, or will it create chains? Will this help my consciousness grow, or will it distract it from its journey?"

Part 4: Guided Meditation: The Angel and the City

Kavi motioned for his students to close their eyes. The muffled sounds of the city—car horns, chatter, distant music—formed a backdrop for his words.

"Take a deep breath," he began, his voice like a soothing current. "And as you breathe in deeply, you might begin to notice a sense of calm spreading through you, as if your body already knows how to relax."

"Picture yourself standing at the edge of a bustling city. The lights are bright, the streets crowded, the air filled with enticing smells and sounds."

"Now, imagine yourself as an angel, radiant and light, walking through this city. Your purpose is clear, your heart full of love."

"As you walk, notice how the sights and sounds tug at you—neon lights flashing, music calling, scents luring you in. You pause at a shop window, the golden glow reflecting in your eyes. A part of you wants to stay, to immerse in the pleasure of the world. But another part remembers—your presence here is not to be lost, but to illuminate.

"You take a breath and place your hand on your heart, feeling the warmth of your own light. As you exhale, you feel a gentle detachment from the distractions around you. They do not disappear, but they lose their power over you. Your love remains, not scattered, but focused—radiating outward.

"You step forward, moving through the city with purpose, neither rejecting nor clinging, simply *being*—a presence of love, free and unbound."

The students' breathing slowed, their faces serene, as if they, too, had become light, walking through the city with renewed clarity.

Conclusion

Kavi's voice broke the stillness, soft but full of power. "Your consciousness is the angel within your temple. Love it, protect it, and guide it wisely. And remember, no matter how long you stay in one place, the path is always there, waiting for you to walk it again."

The students bowed deeply, their hearts full of understanding. As they stepped back into the bustling streets, the world felt different—no less noisy, but clearer, with purpose shining like a beacon ahead."

Affirmations

"I honor my body-temple and guide my consciousness with wisdom, choosing what nourishes my soul over what overstimulates my senses."

"I recognize that love follows where I lead it. I choose to direct my love toward growth, presence, and inner peace."

"I trust myself to return to balance whenever I stray, knowing the path is always waiting for me."

Questions for Further Discussion

1. How does the body's ancient survival instincts sometimes conflict with the needs of our consciousness in the modern world?
2. Can you identify an area of your life where love has transformed into attachment? How might you bring balance to it?
3. What are some overstimulating inputs that may be distorting your natural rhythms of love and awareness?
4. How can you practice being a better gatekeeper of your body-temple without falling into guilt or deprivation?
5. The wizard's watch showed "the eternal now." How can we use this wisdom to free ourselves from unnecessary attachments?

Dancing Buddha's Quote

"Your consciousness is an angel—guide it with love, nourish it with wisdom, and it will lead you to freedom."

STORY 26 – THE PATH TO FREEDOM

The sun rose over the temple of Still Waters, painting the stone courtyard in a golden light that spilled like liquid warmth. Master Ji stood beneath a sprawling cedar tree, his saffron robe flowing gently in the morning breeze. By his side sat a scruffy dog named Tama, her tail wagging lazily as her head rested on her paws.

Across from him sat his two students, Aya and Kento, both in their early twenties. Aya, with her sharp eyes and steady posture, radiated curiosity, while Kento, whose brow often furrowed with deep thought, seemed weighed by unspoken questions.

Tama barked once, startling Kento from his thoughts. Ji chuckled softly. "Even Tama knows it's time to begin."

The students straightened, ready for their lesson.

The Addicted Mind

Ji held up a simple wooden bowl filled with rice. "Tell me," he began, "what would happen if I were to eat only rice and nothing else?"

Aya frowned. "You would grow weak, Master. Rice alone cannot sustain us."

"And if I were to eat too much rice, even when I am no longer hungry?" Ji continued.

Kento nodded, catching on. "You would grow ill. Too much of anything—even something good—can harm us."

Ji smiled. "Indeed. Now consider this: our minds are much like this bowl. They hunger for experience, for sensation. But left unchecked, they can overindulge, consuming more than health requires. This is the nature of the addicted mind."

Aya tilted her head. "But, Master, what of freedom? Should we not have the freedom to choose how much rice to eat, or what to seek for our minds?"

Ji's eyes sparkled with warmth. "Ah, freedom. A word that dances on many tongues but sits uneasily in many hearts. Come with me."

The Journey

Ji led them along a narrow path winding through the temple gardens. Tama trotted alongside, her nose twitching at every scent. The students followed in silence, their senses attuned to the rustling of leaves, the chirping of sparrows, and the distant murmur of a brook.

They came to a small gate leading to an open field where wildflowers bloomed in a riot of color. In the center of the field stood a lone oak tree, its branches stretching wide as if embracing the sky. Ji paused and pointed to the tree.

"This oak is free," he said. "Free to grow tall, to spread its branches, to reach for the sun. But is it free to uproot itself and wander the earth?"

Aya laughed softly. "No, Master. That would go against its nature."

"And if it grew too quickly or too weakly, would it remain standing through the storms?" Ji asked.

Kento shook his head. "No. Its freedom depends on its strength, its health."

Ji knelt beside a patch of wildflowers, cupping one gently in his palm. "So it is with us. True freedom is not the ability to do anything we desire but the ability to live in harmony with our nature. Who would want more freedom than health requires?"

He let the flower go, watching it sway lightly in the breeze. "And yet," he continued, "freedom is not only about our own well-being. Just as this tree is shaped by the sun and the wind, and just as the flower depends on the soil and rain, we too exist in relationship with the world around us. To ask for more freedom than healthy relationships require is to misunderstand freedom itself."

Guided Meditation: The Stream of Balance

Ji led them to a quiet clearing where a small brook flowed over smooth stones. He gestured for them to sit.

"Close your eyes," he said gently. "Take a deep breath. Feel the air moving in, nourishing your body. As you exhale, let go of any tension."

A pause. The sound of the brook surrounded them.

"Imagine yourself as a stream, flowing naturally, effortlessly. The water does not struggle to push uphill, nor does it resist its path. It moves in harmony with the land, nourishing all it touches. This is balance."

A gentle breeze rustled the leaves above them.

"Now, imagine a dam blocking the stream. The water builds up, stagnant, unable to move. This is when we cling too tightly to what is unhealthy."

Another pause.

"Then, imagine the stream rushing too fast, eroding the banks, drowning the roots of the trees that depend on it. This is when we demand more than balance can sustain."

The students breathed deeply, their minds settling.

"Now, let your stream flow just right—steady, gentle, in harmony with all that surrounds it. This is the Middle Way."

He let the silence linger before speaking softly. "When you are ready, open your eyes."

Aya and Kento did so, their faces serene.

Cause and Effect

As they returned to the temple, Ji guided them to the meditation hall. The room was serene, with mats laid out on the floor and sunlight streaming through tall windows. Tama settled in the corner, licking her damp fur.

Ji sat and gestured for his students to do the same. "Close your eyes," he instructed, "and bring to mind a moment when you acted against your health or against the harmony of a relationship. Perhaps you overindulged, avoided responsibility, or clung to something harmful. What were the consequences?"

The students fell into silence. Aya thought of her tendency to overwork herself, ignoring her body's pleas for rest. She recalled the exhaustion, the irritability, the sense of being out of alignment. She also thought of times she pushed too hard in friendships, expecting more than was fair.

Kento's thoughts turned to his struggle with anger. He remembered a heated argument with a friend, the sting of regret, the lingering distance it caused. He also saw how his desire to be completely free of expectations had sometimes hurt those who cared for him.

Ji's voice interrupted their reflections. "Now consider this: were you truly free in those moments, or were you acting from a place of compulsion, of imbalance?"

Aya and Kento both opened their eyes, their faces thoughtful.

"Freedom," Ji said, "is not the absence of restraint but the presence of wisdom. It is the ability to choose the path that leads to health, even when the addicted mind tempts us otherwise. And it is the wisdom to know that freedom is not only about ourselves—it is also about how we give and receive in our relationships."

Affirmations

Ji rose and lit a stick of sandalwood incense, the fragrant smoke curling upward like a prayer.

"I honor the balance that sustains my health."

The students repeated, their voices steady.

"I choose freedom that nurtures both myself and my relationships."

Again, the students echoed his words, the meaning settling deep within them.

Questions for Further Discussion

1. How do you define freedom in your own life? Does it align with Master Ji's teachings?
2. Can you identify areas in your life where you act from compulsion rather than wisdom? How might you begin to change these patterns?
3. How does the concept of the Middle Way apply to your daily decisions?
4. What lessons can you learn from nature about balance and harmony?
5. Do your desires for freedom respect the balance required in relationships?

Dancing Buddha's Quote

"True freedom is the quiet strength to live in harmony with yourself, the world, and the laws that guide all things."

STORY 27 – THE LEAF AND THE ACORN

Introduction

In the heart of an ancient forest, perched on a misty mountainside, sat a serene monastery. It was a place where time moved gently, where the rhythm of life mirrored the whispers of the trees and the murmurs of the streams. Within this haven, Master Soryu, a monk known for his wisdom and calm demeanor, guided his students in the pursuit of understanding life's mysteries.

This is the story of one quiet morning under the oak tree, where a simple question led to profound revelations.

The Leaf

Under the shade of the oak, Master Soryu held a fallen leaf, its green turning to gold with the season's change. Mei, a thoughtful student with bright eyes, broke the silence.

"Master, what happens when we die?"

Haru, her companion, startled at the question, looked up from the forest floor. "Yes, Master. What becomes of us?"

Soryu held up the leaf, letting the sunlight filter through its delicate veins. "Tell me, Mei, is this leaf alive or dead? Where did its consciousness go?"

Mei hesitated. "I suppose it is dead. It has fallen from the tree."

Soryu smiled gently and placed the leaf on the ground. "Let us consider this together. Was the life of this leaf ever truly its own, or was it always the life of the tree, inseparably flowing through every part of it?"

Mei blinked, puzzled. "But the leaf grew, it changed colors, it... seemed alive."

"Indeed it did," Soryu said. "Yet, could it do so without the tree? Could it have existed as a leaf without the roots drawing nourishment from the earth, without the trunk and branches supporting its place in the sunlight?"

Haru leaned forward. "So, the leaf... was never separate from the tree?"

Soryu's eyes twinkled. "Precisely. The leaf was always an extension of the tree, a manifestation of the tree's life. Its form as a leaf was temporary, but its essence was never apart from the tree."

Mei's brow furrowed. "Then, Master, to see the leaf as separate is... a mistake?"

"Not a mistake, my dear," Soryu said kindly. "It is a perspective born of the senses. But look deeper, and you will see that the sense of life was never just in the leaf. It was always the life of the tree, flowing through this form for a time, an inseparable part of the greater whole.

The Journey

Soryu rose and began walking down a path that wound through sun-dappled clearings and shaded thickets. The students followed closely.

"Life," he said, "is like this forest. The trees, the leaves, the streams—each is a unique expression of a single living whole, interconnected and inseparable. To think of a leaf as a separate being is to misunderstand its true nature. Just as the tree and the leaf are one, so too are we part of something greater."

They paused by a sapling, its tiny leaves trembling in the breeze. Soryu picked up an acorn from the ground and held it in his palm. "This acorn contains the potential for a mighty oak. But before it becomes a tree, it must crack open and dissolve. Is this the acorn's end, or is it a transformation?"

"It's a transformation," Mei whispered.

"And when the oak grows tall, do we mourn the acorn?" Soryu asked, his eyes twinkling.

"No, we celebrate it," Haru replied, understanding dawning in his voice.

The Eternal Consciousness

They arrived at a bubbling stream that danced over smooth stones. Soryu gestured for his students to sit on the bank.

"Consider this stream," he said, his voice calm and steady. "Each drop of water flows toward the ocean. When it reaches the ocean, does it cease to exist?"

"No," Mei said. "It becomes the ocean."

"Exactly," Soryu replied. "We are like the drops. When we return to the source, we do not vanish; we expand into the infinite."

Haru's brow furrowed. "But what about fear, Master? Fear of the unknown, of losing ourselves?"

Soryu reached into the stream and lifted a handful of water, letting it fall back. "Fear is like a shadow cast by the mind, an illusion of separateness. The water does not fear becoming the ocean, for it knows it has always been part of it. It knows its journey is part of something greater."

Guided Meditation: Embracing the Eternal

Soryu invited Mei and Haru to close their eyes and listen to the stream. He spoke softly, guiding them into meditation.

"Imagine yourself as a leaf, swaying on a branch. Feel the warmth of the sun, the gentle caress of the wind, and the strength of the tree's connection to the earth flowing through you. When the time comes to let go, feel the freedom in your fall, the trust in the earth that cradles you.

Now see yourself not as the leaf, but as the tree itself. Feel the deep roots grounding you, the branches reaching skyward. The leaves are your expression, each one a unique part of your wholeness. When one leaf falls, you do not diminish; you remain whole, ever-growing, ever-renewing."

Mei felt her heart expand with the imagery, her fears dissolving like mist in the morning sun.

Affirmations

As the meditation ended, Soryu offered affirmations:

I am not separate; I am the wholeness expressing itself in many forms.

I trust the flow of life, knowing every change brings renewal and connection.

Conclusion

As the sun began to set, Soryu and his students walked back to the monastery. Mei carried the acorn they had found, a symbol of transformation and unity. She knelt beside the path and planted it in the soil, Haru helping her cover it gently.

"That acorn," Soryu said, "is a reminder that life is not in the parts, but in the wholeness that creates them. And we are always part of that wholeness."

That evening, Mei and Haru meditated under the stars, the lessons of the day settling deeply into their hearts.

Questions for Further Reflection

1. How does the story of the leaf and the tree change your perspective on life, identity, and the illusion of separateness?

2. In what ways can you see yourself as part of a greater whole in your daily life?
3. How might trusting life's interconnectedness bring peace to your challenges?

Dancing Buddha's Quote

"You are not the leaf; you are the tree expressing itself in countless ways. Trust that your essence is never lost, for it is always part of the infinite whole."

STORY 28 – THE SHARED FLAME

Introduction

In early December, the small mountain town of Whitevale lay blanketed by a fierce snowstorm. The streets, coated in ice and draped in snowdrifts, were still. Houses huddled against the wind like ancient sentinels, their windows glowing faintly in the encroaching twilight. The power flickered but held steady, and the only warmth came from hearth fires crackling behind frosted panes.

High on a hill overlooking the town, the temple of the Dancing Buddha stood steadfast, its red lanterns swaying gently in the wind. Inside, Monk Daran and his three students—Kavi, Anya, and Ravi—gathered around a low, round table near the fire. The room, fragrant with sandalwood and spiced tea, seemed immune to the chaos outside.

Daran looked at his students, their faces lit with the soft orange glow of the flames. "Today," he said, "the lesson comes not from me but from the storm." His voice, calm yet commanding, filled the space like the slow pour of warm honey.

The Roots of the Conflict

Kavi, Anya, and Ravi had been arguing for days. The temple's stores were running low, and each had a different opinion on how best to assist the struggling townsfolk below.

Kavi, with his logical mind, insisted they ration supplies and distribute them strategically. "It's the only efficient way to help as many people as possible," he reasoned.

Anya, her heart ruled by compassion, disagreed. "We must share openly and trust the universe to provide. Withholding anything in a crisis goes against everything we practice here."

Ravi, pragmatic and cautious, proposed they conserve resources for themselves. "If we exhaust our stores, who will help us when the storm worsens?"

The bickering had become relentless. Daran had watched patiently, understanding that the urge to be right often masks something deeper: fear, insecurity, or the desire for validation.

Now, with the storm demanding immediate action, Daran addressed them. "Your arguments hold truth, but they cannot melt snow or feed the hungry. Tonight, we will venture into the town together. Cooperation is our only hope."

The Hidden Fear in Being Right

Bundled in thick robes, they stepped into the storm. Snow swirled around them like restless spirits, muffling their words and forcing them to huddle close. Lanterns flickered in the windows of houses they passed, but the streets were silent, save for the crunch of their boots.

"Kavi," Daran said softly, "what do you feel when Anya and Ravi challenge your ideas?"

Kavi hesitated. "Frustration. I know I'm right, yet they won't listen."

Daran nodded. "And before you were a student here, when else did you feel this need to be right?"

Kavi's expression darkened. "As a child, I had to argue to be heard. My father... he always dismissed me. If I wasn't right, I was ignored."

Daran's gaze softened. "So you learned that being right was not just about truth—it was about being seen."

Kavi swallowed hard, surprised by how deeply the words struck him.

He turned to Anya. "And you, Anya? What stirs in you when Kavi dismisses your approach?"

"Sadness," she admitted. "I feel unheard." She hesitated before adding, "When I was young, I tried to comfort my mother, but no matter what I said, she stayed lost in grief. No amount of love or logic could fix it." She exhaled. "Now, when people reject my kindness, it feels the same—like my voice doesn't matter."

Daran turned to Ravi. "And you?"

Ravi exhaled slowly. "I feel... angry," he confessed. "Growing up, when things were uncertain, my family panicked. I learned that being careful, being cautious, was how you survived. When Kavi and Anya push their ideas, it feels reckless—like they don't see the danger."

Daran nodded, his breath a visible cloud in the icy air. "You each carry a lesson that once kept you safe. But now, it binds you. What if you begin to notice that being right is less about truth and more about a fear you can let go of now? The storm does not argue with the wind; it moves with it, creating something greater."

The students fell silent, pondering his words as the snow deepened.

The Wisdom of the Fire

Arriving in the heart of the town, they found families gathered in the community hall. A large fire blazed in the center, and the air was thick with gratitude as neighbors shared food and warmth.

Daran approached the townsfolk, bowing deeply. "We bring what little we have," he said, unpacking rice, tea, and blankets.

The students worked side by side, their earlier discord melting in the face of shared purpose. Kavi helped organize supplies, his efficiency easing the distribution. Anya comforted frightened children, her compassion a balm to their fears. Ravi stoked the fire, ensuring warmth for everyone.

As the night wore on, the storm raged outside, but within the hall, a profound peace settled.

Guided Meditation: Releasing the Need to Be Right

Daran gathered his students near the fire. "Close your eyes," he said, his voice a steady rhythm. "Let us meditate together."

"Picture the fire before you," Daran began, his voice like a gentle flame itself. "Feel its warmth wrapping around you, inviting a sense of comfort. The fire shares its light effortlessly. It does not hold back, nor does it force itself upon others. It simply is."

The students, eyes closed, breathed deeply.

"Now, see your need to be right as a log in your hands. This log was once a solution—it gave you strength when you needed it. But now, it weighs you down."

A long pause.

"As you place this log into the fire, notice how the flames accept it. The fire does not judge; it transforms. Watch as your old fears dissolve into warmth and light. Let go of needing to win, needing to prove, needing to control."

The room seemed to glow brighter, the fire's crackling harmonizing with the storm's howl outside.

"Repeat silently: *I release the need to be right.*"

A breath.

"And: *I embrace the wisdom of cooperation.*"

The tension within them began to melt away, replaced by peace that felt natural and easy.

The Resolution

By dawn, the storm had passed. Snow still blanketed the town, but the streets were alive with the sound of neighbors digging out together.

As they ascended the hill back to the temple, Daran broke the silence. "What have you learned?"

Kavi spoke first. "That my need to be right came from fear—

fear of failure, of not being enough."

Anya added, "And that listening, truly listening, is an act of courage."

Ravi nodded. "Cooperation doesn't mean giving up our beliefs; it means weaving them together."

Daran smiled. "Exactly. A single flame lights little, but together, they illuminate the darkest nights."

Questions for Reflection

1. Think of a time when you felt the need to be right. What emotions were underneath that urge?
2. Did that need come from an old experience? Was it once a necessary solution?
3. How has that belief served you in the past? How might it be limiting you now?
4. What would happen if, instead of being right, you sought connection?
5. How can you honor both your perspective and the wisdom of others?

Dancing Buddha's Quote

"Wisdom dances not in the triumph of being right, but in the harmony of shared purpose."

STORY 29 – THE MONK AND THE SHAPE OF LOVE

Introduction: A Box of Candy on the Open Sea

The wind danced through the sails, carrying the salty tang of the open sea. The monk and his three students—Maya, Arun, and Leela—stood on the deck of a wooden sailing ship, their robes rippling with the breeze. Around them, the waves lapped gently against the hull, their rhythm steady and calming. The ship had been their home for weeks, a floating classroom for lessons as vast as the ocean itself.

In his hand, the monk held an ornate box of candy. The students watched curiously as he opened it, revealing colorful sweets that glistened in the sunlight.

"Master," Arun asked, "why do your lessons always begin with something so ordinary? A bowl, a chair, now a box of candy? Shouldn't the greatest truths demand something more profound?"

The monk smiled, his gaze soft but steady. "The greatest truths often lie hidden in the simplest things, Arun. In these small, unassuming moments, we find reflections of the infinite. Today, this box of candy will help us explore the nature of emotion and the essence of who we are as conscious love."

He held a piece of candy up to the light. "Tell me," he said, "what do you feel when you see this?"

"It looks delicious," Maya said, her voice filled with anticipation.

"It reminds me of celebrations at home," Leela added, her tone nostalgic.

"And if I were to throw it into the sea before you could taste it?" the monk asked.

Arun frowned. "I would feel frustrated."

The monk nodded. "Emotions, like this candy, take many forms, but they all come from one source: love. Today, we will learn how love, when stretched by attachment, creates the discomforts and over-desires we call emotions."

Section 1: The Thermometer of the Heart

The monk walked to the ship's helm, where a brass thermometer was mounted to measure the sea air. He gestured for the students to gather around. "This thermometer," he said, "is like your heart. It measures temperature, just as your emotions measure the state of your love. You may notice that as the temperature fluctuates, it reflects changes in the environment, just as your emotions reflect the ebb and flow of your attachments and desires.

He dipped the thermometer into a bucket of seawater. "When love is balanced, emotions flow naturally—like the warmth that keeps us comfortable. But when love is stretched or twisted by attachment, it creates extremes—anger, fear, longing. These are not separate from love; they are love bent out of shape."

Maya tilted her head. "But Master, why does love become distorted?"

"Because of attachment, when we cling to something—an idea, a desire, or a memory—we try to shape love to fit our will. This bending creates tension, and that tension becomes emotion. Love is also bent out of shape when we cling to the past or project into the future. Longing for what was or fearing what might be stretches love unnaturally, pulling it away from the present moment where it flows most freely. Yet, even in these distortions, we are never separate from love. We *are* conscious love, always present, always capable of observing and guiding love back into balance. This realization transforms every emotional struggle into a chance to realign with the natural flow of love.""

Section 2: Guided Meditation: The Flow of Love

The monk led the students to the bow of the ship, where heart-shaped pillows were arranged on the wooden deck. The soft green fabric, symbolic of the heart chakra, fluttered slightly in the breeze.

"Now," he said, his voice calm and rhythmic, "let us explore the true shape of love within you. Close your eyes and take a deep breath. Feel the rise and fall of the ship beneath you, like the gentle rhythm of your heart. Bring your awareness to your chest, the center of your heart, and imagine a soft green light glowing there, warm and steady. This is the light of love. Picture a memory or desire that stirs strong emotion within you. See how the light of your heart bends around it, stretching and twisting like rope pulled taut. Notice the discomfort or intensity this creates. Now, imagine the ropes or cords of attachment that hold this memory or desire in place. Visualize these cords gently unraveling, as though cut by a soft blade of light, freeing the energy to flow back into your heart. As the cords dissolve, feel the light flowing freely again, returning to its natural, unbounded shape. With each breath, let the light expand, filling your entire chest with warmth and peace. Repeat silently to yourself: *Love flows freely within me. I release all attachments that distort its truth.*"

The students sat quietly, their breathing slow and steady, as the green light of their hearts filled their awareness. The sound of the waves seemed to harmonize with the soft energy of the meditation, amplifying their sense of release and connection.

The students sat quietly, their breathing slow and steady, as the green light of their hearts filled their awareness. The sound of the waves seemed to harmonize with the soft energy of the meditation, amplifying their sense of release and connection.

Section 3: The Candy of Desire

When the meditation ended, the monk held up the box of candy again. "Tell me," he said, "how did you feel during the meditation?"

Maya smiled. "I felt my love expanding, like it was too big to be contained."

Arun nodded thoughtfully. "And I realized how much my attachments create tension. When I let them go, my emotions felt lighter."

Leela wiped a tear from her cheek. "I thought of a time when I clung to someone's love. It was painful, but I see now that the pain came from my attachment, not from love itself."

The monk handed each of them another piece of candy. "Love, like this candy, is sweet in its pure form. But when we attach to it, we demand that it always taste the same, look the same, or stay with us forever. Holding onto what love was or trying to control what it should be bends it out of shape, creating tension and discomfort. However, when we remember that we are conscious love—aware and present—we can see these distortions not as failures but as opportunities to adjust. Love thrives in the present moment, where it moves freely, adapting and expanding without force."

Section 4: The Thermometer's Lesson

The monk dipped the thermometer into the sea, showing how the mercury shifted with the water's temperature. "When love contracts through fear or loss, it feels cold—like sadness or isolation. And yet, this coldness is not permanent. It is an invitation to notice where you are clinging or afraid to let go. Similarly, when love expands too rapidly through over-desire or anger, it burns. These extremes are not love's fault; they are signals to rebalance."

He then placed the thermometer in the sunlight, where it rose quickly. "When love expands too rapidly through over-desire or anger, it burns. These extremes are not love's fault; they are the result of attachments pushing love out of balance."

Arun spoke, his voice steady. "So our emotions are not wrong, Master. They are signals, like the thermometer, showing us when love is being bent."

"Exactly," the monk said. "Emotions are messengers, revealing where love has been stretched or bent by attachment. When you feel anger, ask yourself: What attachment am I defending? When you feel sadness, ask: What love am I afraid to lose? And when you feel longing, ask: Am I clinging to the past or reaching for a future that hasn't arrived? The answers to these questions will gently guide you back to the present, where love flows freely and balance is restored."

Affirmations

"Love flows freely within me. I release all attachments that distort its truth."

"I honor my emotions as messengers, guiding me back to balance and love."

Conclusion: Returning to Love's True Shape

As the sun began to set, the students sat quietly on the deck, each holding a piece of candy. The monk looked at them with warmth. "Love is the only emotion," he said. "When it bends, it creates discomfort or desire. But when it flows freely, it fills us with peace."

The students nodded, their hearts lighter. They watched the sun dip below the horizon, the sea glowing with the soft hues of twilight. The lesson of love's true shape stayed with them, a quiet compass guiding their inner seas.

Questions for Reflection

1. Think of a recent emotion that felt overwhelming. What attachment might have bent your love out of shape?
2. How can you use your emotions as signals to return to love's true flow?
3. What practices help you release attachments and nurture the natural shape of love within you?

Dancing Buddha's Quote

"Love is the light that bends to fill every space. When it stretches too far, it asks only to flow freely again."

STORY 30 – NOURISHING THE PATH WITH INTENTION

The Echo of the Question

Under the silver glow of the full moon, the village by the sea buzzed with excitement. The Festival of Abundance was in full swing, with laughter, music, and the aroma of a grand feast swirling through the air. It was a night of celebration, of gratitude, of life itself.

Master Sona's students, Ravi and Mira, followed him through the bustling square, their eyes wide at the colorful spread before them. Platters of vibrant fruits, golden roasted vegetables, steaming rice, and savory meats filled the tables, a tapestry of colors and scents.

Mira's eyes lingered on a platter of roasted lamb, the glaze glistening under the lantern light. A question pressed at her heart. Turning to her teacher, she whispered, "Master, is it right to eat meat? To take life for our nourishment?"

Sona's eyes softened, his gaze steady. "That question," he said, "is an echo in every heart. But the answer is not found here"—he gestured to the feast—"it is found here." His fingers touched his chest, just above his heart. "The way we choose to nourish ourselves is the way we choose to walk our path. Tonight, let us explore this together."

His words wrapped around them, soft as silk, lingering in the air as they moved through the festival.

The Question of Nourishment and Purpose

As the moon climbed higher, Sona gathered his students beneath the ancient banyan tree. Its branches reached out like a protective embrace, the leaves whispering softly in the breeze.

"Look around," Sona began, his voice low and steady. "Feel the earth beneath you. Notice the air on your skin. Hear the whisper of the leaves." His words paced their awareness, grounding them in the present moment.

"Tell me," he continued, "What do you see when you look at the food before you?"

Mira glanced at the platters of fruits and grains. "I see life... given freely by the earth."

Ravi hesitated, his eyes on the roasted lamb. "I see... death," he said softly, his shoulders slumping. "A life taken."

Sona's voice remained calm, matching their emotions, leading them forward. "And what does that mean—to take in life? Is one path more sacred than another?"

Mira's brow furrowed. "The fruit is given freely. The tree lives on. But the lamb... it will not breathe again."

Sona nodded. "Yet, does the fruit not also grow, reach for the sun, drink from the rain? Is its life any less? When we consume, whether plant or animal, we are not choosing between life and death. We are choosing *how* we honor what we take in."

His voice softened. "To eat is to take life in some form. The question is not what we consume, but whether we do so with purpose—with gratitude, respect, and understanding."

Mira and Ravi exchanged glances.

"Close your eyes," Sona instructed. "Imagine a single grain of rice growing... stretching toward the sun. Feel its roots in the earth, the water that feeds it. Can you sense the quiet pulse of its life?"

They closed their eyes, guided by his voice.

"Now, imagine yourself taking that rice into your body. Feel how it nourishes you, becomes part of you. The life it carried now fuels your steps, your thoughts, your purpose."

A breath passed. Mira's fingers tingled. "I feel it," she whispered.

Sona smiled. "Everything we consume—food, knowledge, even emotions—becomes part of us. If we take without awareness, we walk without awareness. But when we receive with gratitude, we align with our purpose."

The Fields of Choice

Under the moonlit sky, Sona led them along the winding path to the fields. Rows of vegetables stood tall, their leaves rustling softly.

He bent down and pulled a carrot from the soil, the roots tearing from the earth. "Life, given," he said, holding it up. "And life, transformed."

Mira touched the rough skin of the carrot. "Even this?"

Sona nodded. "Even this. It lived, it grew, and now, it gives." He turned the carrot in his hands. "The way we take in life mirrors the way we give back. If we nourish ourselves mindlessly, we live mindlessly. If we receive with gratitude, we act with purpose."

His voice became a whisper, flowing like the night breeze. "With each meal, we make a choice—not only about what we eat, but about the kind of person we wish to be. Do we take in only for ourselves, or do we consume in a way that strengthens our purpose? Do we waste, or do we use every moment to nourish something greater?"

Mira and Ravi stood in silence, feeling the weight of the question settle into their bones.

Guided Meditation: The Sacred Offering

Under a blooming jacaranda tree, Sona gestured for them to sit. "Close your eyes. Feel the earth supporting you."

His voice was slow, rhythmic, hypnotic.

"Imagine you are a tree. Your roots reach deep, drinking from the soil. Your branches stretch wide, embracing the sky. You take in, and you give in return."

A pause.

"Now, see the fruit ripening on your branches, full of life. When it falls, it feeds the earth, feeds others. Life flows through you, endlessly."

Another pause.

"Now, imagine the choices you make. Each bite of food, each thought, each action—what do you nourish? What do you give back?"

His voice softened. "The way you eat is the way you walk your path. Do you consume mindlessly, or do you receive with purpose? Do you take from life, or do you dance with it?"

A silence stretched, deep and full.

The Lesson of Intentional Living

By dawn, the festival had ended, but the lesson remained.

As they walked back to the temple, Sona spoke. "Every day, we nourish ourselves—not just with food, but with thoughts, actions, and emotions. What we take in shapes the steps we walk. To consume with awareness is to walk with intention."

Mira and Ravi nodded, their hearts lighter.

Sona smiled. "To honor life is not about what you choose to eat. It is about how you choose to live."

Affirmations

"With each choice I make, I nourish the path I walk."

"I receive life with gratitude and walk my path with intention."

Questions for Further Discussion

1. How do your daily choices—food, thoughts, actions—reflect your deeper purpose?

2. What does it mean to take in life with gratitude and awareness?
3. Think of a time you consumed something without mindfulness. How did it affect your energy and path?
4. How can the practice of mindful nourishment extend beyond food into the way you engage with the world?
5. What are some ways you can bring more purpose into everyday habits, making even the simplest actions meaningful?
6.

Dancing Buddha's Quote

"To eat with awareness is to dance with life. To consume with gratitude is to honor the sacred flow."

PART FOUR

Purpose

Gregory K. Cadotte

PART FOUR

PURPOSE – WALKING THE PATH WITH INTENTION

Purpose. It's a word that carries immense weight, often whispered in moments of quiet reflection or shouted in frustration when life feels directionless. As you sit here now, reading these words, you may find yourself remembering times when you longed for clarity—perhaps a moment in the past, or even a feeling arising now. And that's perfectly natural, isn't it? Because the search for purpose is not a straight road; it is a journey of discovery, shaped as much by the questions we ask as the answers we find.

As you continue reading, you may notice a sense of curiosity beginning to grow—a willingness to explore the essence of purpose through stories and meditations that illuminate what it means to walk the path with intention. Purpose is not about striving toward some distant, external goal; it is about living authentically, aligning your actions with your values, and realizing that the path itself is the destination.

Imagine standing at the base of a mountain shrouded in mist. As you take a deep breath, feeling the ground beneath your feet, you may become aware of the uncertainty before you. You know there is a peak somewhere above, but the path to reach it is unclear. Do you wait for the fog to lift, or do you take the first step, trusting that clarity will come as you move forward?

Your unconscious mind already knows that purpose often unfolds like this—a journey through mist, where each step reveals more of the path ahead. Some moments may feel uncertain, yet as you move forward, new insights emerge. The stories ahead will introduce seekers like yourself—people who, like you, may have once hesitated in uncertainty but found their way by trusting the journey.

And perhaps, even now, a part of you is beginning to sense the truth in this: **Clarity comes not before the journey, but because of it.**

But purpose is not only about big moments or grand revelations. It is shaped in the smallest of choices—the food we eat, the way we listen, the way we honor the life we have been given. Every act is an offering to our path. With each breath, each step, we are shaping who we become.

The stories in this section remind us that we do not need perfect certainty to move forward. Purpose is nourished by the way we engage with life—with awareness, with gratitude, and with an open heart.

The Importance of Authenticity

As you sit comfortably now, you might allow yourself to reflect: *Have there been times when you felt the need to wear a mask, to fit into expectations that weren't truly yours?* It's natural. We all do it at times. Yet deep within, there is a part of you—your most authentic self—that knows real purpose cannot thrive in inauthenticity.

The more you embrace your true self, the more naturally you begin to align with your purpose. And as you consider this, imagine a student who once believed their worth was tied to external validation. They sought approval, shaped themselves to fit the expectations of others, and yet... something inside felt distant, disconnected.

Then, a moment came—perhaps it was small, perhaps it was profound—when they realized that their true power lay not in pleasing others, but in aligning with their own values. This shift, this profound realization, is something your mind can begin to integrate now, in your own way, at your own pace.

Perhaps, in the days ahead, you'll notice subtle ways in which authenticity feels more natural. And as that happens, you might find yourself experiencing more ease, more flow—just as you were meant to.

Purpose as a Living Practice

Purpose is not a static destination; it is a dynamic force, a living practice. Some people believe they must wait for a single defining moment to uncover their purpose, but what if purpose is something that emerges naturally, moment by moment?

As you sit here now, you might already begin to sense how purpose is like a compass—always available, always guiding, even when the terrain changes. And just as a compass does not dictate the landscape but offers direction, your purpose adapts with you.

Imagine now: A steady flame, unwavering, even when winds of doubt or distraction blow. That flame exists within you. And as you allow that image to settle into your awareness, notice how it strengthens, how it steadies. Each choice, each action aligned with your values, feeds that flame, making it even brighter.

The meditations in this section will help you reconnect with this inner compass. And as you engage with them, you might find yourself naturally drawn toward a deeper sense of alignment, with curiosity rather than pressure, with openness rather than expectation. And that's a wonderful thing, isn't it?

Alignment Brings Peace

One of the most profound outcomes of aligning with your purpose is the deep peace it brings. You've likely felt this before, even if only for a moment—that effortless sense of flow when your actions match your deepest values. It feels natural, doesn't it? Like a river moving freely, carving its way with ease. And just like a river, when blocked or diverted, tension builds. The same is true for you.

Yet, the more you align, the more naturally your energy flows. And as that happens, struggles transform into opportunities, obstacles into lessons. Imagine a moment in your future—perhaps days, perhaps weeks from now—where you experience that alignment so deeply that even challenges feel like part of the journey. That moment is already waiting for you.

And when it arrives, you may smile to yourself, recognizing that all along, your purpose was guiding you here.

An Invitation to Begin

As you prepare to read the stories and engage in the meditations ahead, I invite you to allow yourself to explore them not just with your conscious mind, but with your whole being. You don't need to have all the answers right now. In fact, it's in releasing that need that the most profound discoveries unfold naturally.

What does purpose mean to you? Perhaps, as you reflect on this question, your mind opens to new insights. There is no right or wrong answer—only the truth of your experience.

And as you walk this path with intention, may you find not only your purpose but also the joy and fulfillment that come from living in alignment with your deepest truth.

Affirmations

> *"My actions align with my inner truth, and I trust the path to unfold in its own perfect time."*

> *"My purpose flows naturally from within, guiding me with clarity and peace."*

> *"Every step I take reveals more of the journey, and I walk forward with confidence and ease."*

Through the stories and practices ahead, may you discover the steady flame of your own intention—guiding, unwavering, always illuminating the way toward a life lived with purpose and authenticity.

STORY 31 – THE PATH AND THE BLINDNESS

Introduction

On the bustling streets of Las Vegas, where neon lights flicker against the night sky and the rhythmic clinking of slot machines hums through the air, stood an unassuming monastery. The sign above its modest door read Inner Path Temple, though locals fondly called it the "Street Monastery."

Within its walls, far removed from the city's distractions, Brother Michael guided seekers toward deeper truths. Unlike the flashing billboards and promises of instant gratification outside, his lessons unfolded quietly—like whispers to the soul, planting seeds of awareness in those who were ready.

Among his students were three young seekers: Lisa, a fiery attorney struggling to balance ambition with inner peace; Jake, a musician caught between his passion for art and his need for recognition; and Mia, a nurse who had spent her life healing others but had forgotten how to care for herself.

One bright evening, Brother Michael gathered them for a lesson—one that would shift their perspectives forever.

Section 1: The Mystery of the Mouse

The students sat cross-legged on the temple's worn wooden floor, forming a circle around Brother Michael. In the center lay a small wooden box, carved with delicate swirling patterns. The candlelight flickered, making the carvings seem almost alive.

Brother Michael picked up a bronze figurine—a mouse clutching a tiny golden key—and held it up with a quiet smile.

"Tonight, we explore the nature of belief. And perhaps, as you listen, you may find yourself beginning to notice something new... something that has always been there, just waiting to be seen."

He cradled the figurine in his hands and began:

"Once, in an ancient kingdom, a small mouse discovered a golden key. The mouse, convinced that this key would unlock a door to endless treasures, devoted its life to searching for that door. It scurried through villages, tunnels, and forests, tirelessly seeking its prize. Years passed, and the mouse found nothing. Exhausted, it finally paused... and looked around. And for the first time, it noticed the world—the golden hues of sunlight filtering through the trees, the whispers of the wind through the grass, the quiet rhythm of life unfolding in every direction. And in that moment, the mouse realized: 'I am not the seeker of treasures... I am the one who holds the key.'"

A silence settled over the room.

Lisa frowned slightly. "Are you saying our beliefs blind us?"

Brother Michael's eyes twinkled. "Beliefs can be powerful guides. But when we hold onto them too tightly, they become cages. Like the mouse, we become so focused on what we are searching for that we forget to see the beauty of the journey itself.

"And when you think about it... what happens when you stop searching for treasure... and start noticing the treasure that's already around you?"

Lisa inhaled sharply. The room felt different now, as if something unseen had shifted.

Section 2: The Light of Many Colors

To deepen the lesson, Brother Michael led the students to the rooftop, where the city's neon glow stretched endlessly. Below, people moved through the streets, lost in their own stories—their own pursuits of fortune, pleasure, or escape.

"Close your eyes," he instructed.

"And as you do, you might begin to notice how easily your breath slows... how effortlessly your body begins to relax... how naturally your mind opens, just a little more than before."

"Now, imagine a bright light forming at the center of your being. A light shimmering with every color imaginable. It is not bound by form or belief—it simply is. Let it expand, growing warmer, freer, more radiant with every breath.

"And as this light expands, you may begin to notice... how easily old thoughts begin to dissolve. The idea that you must always win. The belief that you must heal everyone. The thought that your worth is tied to achievement.

"Watch them crumble... and as they do, the space within and around you expands. And you don't have to do anything... just allow yourself to experience what is already here."

Jake let out a slow breath. "It feels like I'm floating."

Mia's voice trembled. "I see colors blending together... and it's beautiful."

Brother Michael nodded. "This light is your essence—a loving awareness that does not need to be defined, controlled, or confined. Beliefs are tools, not masters. The moment we define ourselves by them, we stop seeing the infinite possibilities beyond them."

Section 3: The Open Field and the Crossroads

Back in the temple, Brother Michael guided them into another meditation.

"Imagine yourself standing at a crossroads. To one side, there is a paved road—familiar, structured, predictable. It is the path built from your strongest beliefs, the one you've followed for years. It feels safe."

"Now, take a step back and turn around. Behind you lies something else—a vast, open field, stretching endlessly in all directions. There is no road, no path, no boundary."

"And as you step into this field, you may begin to notice... a lightness in your body. A sense of freedom opening up inside you. The realization that you are not confined by the road, that you never were."

Lisa's breath hitched. When she opened her eyes, tears streamed down her face. "I've been so caught up in winning arguments, proving myself, fighting for control... that I forgot what it feels like to just be."

Jake nodded. "It's like I've been playing the same song over and over, afraid to change the melody. But the field... it's full of new possibilities."

Mia exhaled. "I've held onto the belief that I must heal everyone. But now, I see that... I need to let go of control. Healing happens in its own time, not by my will alone."

Section 4: The Dancing Buddha

Brother Michael led them outside to a statue of the Dancing Buddha in the temple courtyard. The statue's posture exuded motion, fluidity, and joy.

"The Dancing Buddha teaches us that true freedom is not about clinging to a single path... but about moving with life's rhythm—unbound, open, ever-evolving."

"And what if, right now, you could begin to move with that rhythm? What if, in the days ahead, you find yourself... more open, more present, more aware of the dance that is always within you?"

Conclusion and Affirmations

The students left the monastery that night, their hearts lighter, their minds clearer.

"I am not my beliefs; I am the loving awareness beyond them."

"I embrace the freedom to dance with life, unbound and open."

Questions for Further Discussion:

1. What beliefs in your life have acted like the mouse's key—guiding you but also limiting what you see?
2. When was the last time you paused to step off your familiar path and notice the "open field" of new possibilities? What did you discover?
3. In what areas of your life are you trying to control the rhythm instead of dancing with it? How can you begin to trust the flow more?
4. If you could release just one belief today that no longer serves you, what would it be? How would that shift your life?

Dancing Buddha's Quote

"The dance of life begins where the path ends. Let go of the map... and you'll find the field where freedom resides."

STORY 32 – THE SOIL OF MINDFUL LIVING

Introduction

In a quiet mountain monastery nestled between mist-laden peaks, Master Sarva sat in stillness by a lotus pond. Snowflakes fell softly, their delicate dance mirroring the serene hum of the nearby stream. This was a place of reflection, where life moved at the pace of breath, and every moment carried the weight of meaning.

Three students—Arin, Mira, and Kavi—approached Sarva, their breaths visible in the crisp air. They carried a question that had lingered in their minds, one they had debated throughout the morning.

"Master," Arin began, kneeling before him, "we have been

discussing the nature of food and nourishment. Some believe we should eat only what nature offers freely—fruits, beans, and nuts. Others argue that we should consume whatever sustains us, regardless of its source. What should we eat?"

Sarva opened his eyes, their gaze as deep as the forest surrounding them. He let the question settle in the stillness before speaking. "Bring me the cup."

The Cup and Its Purpose

Kavi hurried to fetch it—a simple earthen vessel adorned with a painted flower. He handed it to Sarva, who held it up, letting snowflakes settle gently on its surface.

"This cup, though humble, carries both beauty and purpose," Sarva said, turning it slowly in his hands. "Tell me, what should we fill it with?"

"Water, Master," Mira suggested, her voice thoughtful.

"Tea," said Arin, his practicality showing.

"Whatever is needed," Kavi added softly.

Sarva smiled faintly. "So it is with our bodies. They, too, are cups—crafted by nature to carry life. What we fill them with must serve both our needs and the harmony of the world. Come, let us walk."

A Path Through Snow and Thought

The group wandered into the forest, the snow falling lightly around them. The rare phenomenon cloaked the trees in shimmering white, and their steps crunched softly beneath their feet.

Mira stopped by a tree bearing late-season persimmons and plucked one, offering it to Sarva. "Is this what we should eat, Master? It seems perfect—nature's gift," she said.

Sarva accepted the fruit but did not eat it. Instead, he held it gently, observing its bright orange color and smooth surface. "Tell me, Mira, do you think this fruit lives?"

She hesitated. "It was alive, but now it is not. Its purpose is to nourish."

Sarva placed the persimmon in the cup, letting snowflakes settle around it. "Everything lives, Mira. Even this persimmon. Its journey from tree to hand to mouth is an end, but also a beginning. When you eat, remember this: all consumption ends the lives of something. To eat with respect is to honor the lives that sustain us."

The Seed in the Earth

Arin, the most pragmatic of the three, frowned. "But Master, if all consumption ends lives, does that not mean we are free to eat anything? Meat, plants, or even indulgent feasts? Does it truly matter?"

Sarva stopped and gestured for them to sit by the base of an ancient oak tree. He reached into his robe and withdrew a tiny seed, holding it delicately between his fingers.

"This seed," he said, "contains the promise of a tree. But for that promise to be fulfilled, the seed must be placed in fertile soil, given water, and touched by the sun. If neglected, it will wither. Your body and mind are like this seed."

Kavi tilted his head. "How so, Master?"

Sarva placed the seed on the snow-covered ground. "What

you consume is the soil that surrounds the seed. If you nourish it with wisdom—eating only what sustains and strengthens—it will grow into something magnificent. But if you overindulge, or feed it poorly, the seed will struggle, and its potential will remain unfulfilled."

He lifted the seed again, warming it between his palms. "When we eat, we must ask: does this food enrich the soil of our lives? Does it nurture the seed of our purpose?"

Guided Meditation: Nurturing the Seed Within

Sarva invited the students to sit quietly under the oak tree. "Close your eyes," he said, his voice soft and steady. "Take a deep breath, feeling the cool air filling your lungs. Let your exhale carry away any tension, as though releasing a weight you no longer need."

The students followed, their breaths becoming slower, steadier.

"Now," Sarva continued, "imagine within you a small seed—a seed full of infinite potential. See its delicate shell, feel its presence within you. Notice the soil surrounding it. Perhaps it is rich and alive, or maybe it feels dry, needing care. With each breath, imagine the soil becoming warmer, richer, more nourishing."

He paused, letting the image settle in their minds.

"As you breathe in, feel the sunlight streaming down, warming the soil. With each exhale, imagine water flowing gently into the earth, bringing life. Repeat silently: 'I nourish the seed of my purpose with every mindful choice.'"

The students sat in stillness, the image vivid and alive within them.

The Weight of a Choice

Sarva opened his eyes and spoke again. "Let me tell you a story, one that came from the Buddha himself, one that may trouble you but carries great truth."

The forest seemed to hold its breath as he began.

"There was once a couple, poor and starving, who traveled across a barren land. Along the way, their child died. Desperate to survive, they made the unthinkable choice to eat their own child's flesh. Each bite, they wept. When they reached safety, they vowed never to eat again for pleasure or habit—but only to sustain life."

The students' faces paled. Mira's voice trembled. "Master, why would you tell us such a story?"

"To teach you this," Sarva said gently, "that to eat mindlessly, for pleasure or distraction, is no less grave than their choice. Every bite we take, whether of flesh or fruit, ends a life. When we eat, we must ask if the life we consume is honored by its purpose—to fuel our growth, to sustain our practice, to nurture our seed."

The Final Test

As the snow began to subside, Sarva handed the cup to Mira. "Take this cup back to the monastery and fill it with whatever you believe would best nourish us."

Mira hesitated, the weight of the task clear on her face. She bowed deeply. "Yes, Master."

Along the way, she picked a persimmon from the tree, mindful of its weight in her hands. At the monastery, she added a few beans, a handful of nuts, and a single drop of honey.

When she presented it to Sarva, he examined the offering and smiled. "You have understood well. This is enough to nourish the body and honor the earth. Mindful eating is not only in the act but in the intention."

Affirmations for Mindful Nourishment

As the students sat down to share the simple meal, Sarva spoke two final affirmations:

"I nourish the soil of my life with every choice I make."

"I honor the lives that sustain me by taking only what I need."

Conclusion

Above, the sun broke through the clouds, illuminating the snowy landscape with warmth. The students ate slowly, savoring each bite as if it were a prayer. They felt not only nourished but connected—to the food, to the earth, and to the wisdom of their master.

And in the quiet of the forest monastery, Sarva's teachings settled into their hearts, like seeds waiting to bloom.

Questions for Further Discussion

1. How does the metaphor of the seed deepen your understanding of mindful eating?
2. What choices can you make to nourish the "soil" of your life?
3. How can the affirmation "I nourish the seed of my purpose" guide your daily actions?
4. What does it mean to honor the lives that sustain your own?

Dancing Buddha's Quote

"The seed holds infinite potential, but only the soil of mindful choices can bring it to life."

Gregory K. Cadotte

STORY 33 – THE DANCE OF UNDERSTANDING

Introduction

The monastery stood atop a quiet mountain, its silhouette etched against the morning mist. Within its serene walls, Master Kiran, a monk with a gaze as deep as the ocean, taught his students not with lectures but through moments of living wisdom. Among them, Sohan, Priya, and Anil were eager learners, each carrying their unique struggles.

Sohan, the most anxious, struggled with a deep fear of failure. One morning, as they swept the temple courtyard, he approached Kiran.

"Master," Sohan said, his voice tinged with frustration, "every task you give me feels like a test, and I fail so often. How can I ever reach understanding?"

Kiran paused, leaning on his broom. "Come, Sohan. Let us take a walk."

The Empty Vase

They walked to a shed where Kiran retrieved a simple clay vase and placed it in Sohan's hands.

"This vase is your task," Kiran said. "Fill it with water from the stream below and bring it back here without spilling a drop."

Sohan hurried to the stream, filled the vase to its brim, and began climbing the rocky path. Each step caused water to slosh over the sides. By the time he returned, the vase was nearly empty.

"I failed," Sohan said, lowering his head.

Kiran smiled and held the vase. "Did you? What did you learn?"

Sohan hesitated. "To walk more carefully."

"Good," Kiran said. "Go again."

This time, Sohan moved slower, shielding the vase with his hands. Yet a sudden gust of wind caused him to stumble, spilling more water. He returned with even less.

"What did you learn this time?"

"That I must guard the vase from the wind," Sohan replied.

"Then go again," Kiran said with calm encouragement.

Hour after hour, Sohan repeated the task. Each time, he learned—to balance his steps, to steady his grip, to anticipate the wind. Finally, he returned with the vase full, its surface rippling but undisturbed.

"Master, I did it!" he exclaimed.

Kiran chuckled. "Yes, but would you have succeeded without the spills and stumbles?"
"No," Sohan admitted. "Each mistake taught me."
"And that," Kiran said, "is the dance of understanding. Each step, even a misstep, leads you closer to mastery."

The Ink and the Calligraphy

The next day, Kiran handed Sohan a brush and parchment. "Write the character for 'peace,'" he instructed.
Sohan dipped the brush and made his first stroke. It wavered, uneven and clumsy. Frustrated, he crumpled the parchment and tried again. Each attempt seemed worse than the last. "I can't do it!" Sohan shouted, throwing down the brush.
Kiran picked up a discarded parchment. "Look here," he said, pointing to the lines. "Your strokes have grown steadier. Do you see the improvement?"
Sohan examined the pages, realizing the subtle progress. His frustration softened into curiosity.
"Why didn't you stop me when I became angry?" he asked.
"Because anger is a step in the dance," Kiran replied. "It teaches patience. Now, try again, not to achieve perfection but to learn from each stroke."
This time, Sohan approached the task differently. Each stroke became an experiment, each page a new beginning. By evening, the character for 'peace' appeared balanced and elegant. "There is no failure, Sohan," Kiran said. "Only process. Each act shapes you into who you are becoming."

Guided Meditation: The River of Learning

That evening, Kiran led his students to the edge of a quiet river.

"Close your eyes," he said softly.

"Imagine yourself standing in this river. The water flows gently around you, carrying leaves, pebbles, and even debris. Each piece represents a moment of learning—a success, a mistake, a challenge. Notice how the river does not cling to anything. It moves freely, carrying everything forward.

Now, let your mind be the river. Welcome each experience. Let the lessons flow through you without resistance. Feel the calm of accepting all parts of your journey."

The students' breaths slowed as they sank into the imagery, their hearts lighter with understanding.

The Journey and the Stone

Weeks later, Kiran and his students traveled to a nearby village. The path was treacherous, winding through dense forests and rocky terrain. Along the way, Sohan tripped on a jagged stone and scraped his knee.

"Why must the path be so difficult?" he grumbled.

Kiran picked up the stone and handed it to him. "What do you see?"

Sohan studied it closely. "Rough edges... but also intricate patterns."

"Challenges are like this stone," Kiran said. "At first, they seem like obstacles. But look deeper, and you see their beauty. Without them, we would remain untested and unformed."

Sohan carried the stone for a while, letting its weight remind him of the lesson. When they reached the village, he handed it back to Kiran. "The path didn't change," Sohan said, "but I did." Kiran nodded. "That is the essence of understanding. Each step transforms you."

Conclusion: The Dance of Life

Back at the monastery, Sohan reflected on his journey. Tasks that once felt burdensome now seemed like opportunities. He saw each moment—whether tending the garden, meditating, or writing calligraphy—as a step in the dance of understanding.

One evening, as the sun set behind the mountains, Sohan approached Kiran.

"Master, I see it now. There is no failure, only learning. Each act, whether graceful or clumsy, adds to the rhythm of life."

Kiran's eyes gleamed. "Yes, Sohan. Life is a dance. As long as you keep moving, there is no end to what you can become."

Under the vast sky, master and student sat in silence, their hearts at peace, knowing the dance would continue with every sunrise.

Affirmations

"Each step I take, whether faltering or steady, brings me closer to understanding."

"I embrace every challenge as a lesson, allowing myself to grow."

Questions for Reflection

1. Think of a recent challenge you faced. What lessons did it carry for you?
2. How can you reframe mistakes as steps in your personal dance of growth?
3. In what areas of life can you practice patience and persistence today?

Dancing Buddha's Quote

"Life is not a test to pass but a rhythm to embrace. Each step, whether graceful or stumbled, adds to the beauty of the dance."

STORY 34 – THE CANDLE'S FLAME

Introduction

In the heart of London, Ontario, nestled between the bustle of Richmond Row and the serenity of the Thames River, stood a small Vietnamese monastery called Windlight Zen Temple. New to the city, the monastery was a sanctuary of mindfulness amid the hum of urban life.

The temple's abbot, Master Soryu, was known for his gentle wisdom and knack for making ancient teachings accessible in modern settings. Three devoted students—Kael, Amara, and Jorin—frequented the temple, drawn by its peaceful atmosphere and their master's transformative lessons.

One crisp autumn morning, as the wind carried the scent of

fallen leaves and distant traffic, Master Soryu gathered his students in the temple's quiet courtyard. Today, he intended to teach them a profound truth about living with purpose and love.

The Candle's Lesson

Master Soryu stood in the courtyard, holding a slender candle. Its flame flickered gently in the breeze. "This candle," he began, his voice calm yet resonant, "holds a lesson for us all. It is the light of your heart—your love, compassion, and joy. Our task today is to discover how to keep this flame alive."

Kael, the youngest student, leaned forward eagerly. "Master, how can such a small flame teach us something so big?"

The master's eyes twinkled. "This small flame contains all the wisdom you need. Walk too fast, and it flickers. Walk too slow, and it may extinguish. How we walk, sit, talk, listen, and act determines whether this flame endures or fades. Let's begin."

The Streets of London: A Test of Pace

Master Soryu handed each student a lit candle and led them out of the monastery and into the streets of downtown London. The contrast between the temple's tranquility and the city's vibrant energy was palpable. Cars honked, cyclists whizzed by, and pedestrians hurried along Dundas Street.

"Observe the pace of the world around you," Master Soryu instructed. "What do you notice?"

Amara, the most reflective of the three, observed, "Everything moves so quickly. People rush from place to place without pause."

Master Soryu nodded. "And what happens to their flames?"

"They flicker," Jorin replied, his tone thoughtful. "Or maybe they don't even realize they've gone out."

As they walked, the students experienced the challenge of keeping their flames alive. Kael, curious and impulsive, walked too quickly, and his flame was soon extinguished by a gust of wind. "Master, my flame is gone," he said, his voice tinged with disappointment.

"This," Master Soryu said gently, "is what happens when we let urgency dictate our pace. The wind of life will always be there. But if we rush, we cannot protect our light."

Amara, trying to avoid Kael's mistake, slowed her pace dramatically. She lingered so much that her flame dimmed and went out. "I was too careful," she admitted, her face clouded with self-doubt.

"The flame requires attention, not hesitation," the master explained. "Walking too slowly is as unbalanced as moving too fast."

Jorin, who had long practiced the art of mindfulness, kept his flame steady. "I focus on the candle and adjust to the wind," he said when Master Soryu asked how he succeeded.

The master smiled. "Exactly. The flame is your love. It thrives when you are present, moving at its natural pace—not rushing ahead or lagging behind."

The Candle as a Way of Being

As they returned to the monastery, the master invited the students to reflect on the lesson in a broader sense. Sitting in the meditation hall, the scent of sandalwood filling the air, Master

Soryu asked, "Do you see how this applies not just to walking, but to every aspect of life?"

The students looked thoughtful.

"To walk at the pace of love," the master continued, "is to live at the pace of love. This means we walk, sit, talk, listen, and act with the same care we give the flame. But there are other paces as well."

Kael raised an eyebrow. "Other paces?"

Master Soryu nodded. "We can walk at the pace of kindness, where each step is a gesture of care for others. Or at the pace of cooperation, where we move in harmony with those around us. There is the pace of patience, which allows us to let life unfold naturally, and the pace of gratitude, where every step is a quiet acknowledgment of what we've been given."

Amara's eyes lit up. "So, the pace we choose reflects what we carry within us?"

"Exactly," the master replied. "When we align our pace with states like love, kindness, or cooperation, we sustain the flame within us and brighten the world around us."

The Meditation of the Flame

The master then led a guided meditation to deepen the lesson. He placed a single candle in the center of the hall and invited the students to close their eyes.

"Breathe deeply," he said, his voice a calm current. "Feel the rhythm of your breath—steady, effortless, like the flame's glow. Imagine a candle within your heart. Its flame burns warm and golden, unaffected by time or distraction."

The students inhaled and exhaled, the imagery of the flame steadying their thoughts.

"Now, picture yourself moving through your day," the master continued. "You are walking—not too fast, not too slow—feeling the flame steady within you. See yourself speaking gently, listening with your whole being, and acting with compassion. Each moment, the flame remains bright, because you honor its pace."

After a long pause, Master Soryu added two affirmations for them to carry:

"I move at the pace of love, allowing my light to guide me."

"My actions flow from compassion, steady and true."

The students repeated the affirmations softly, their voices harmonizing with the flicker of the candle.

The Final Test: Acting at the Pace of Love

The master concluded the day with a challenge. Each student was given a new candle and asked to carry it through their daily lives—on walks, during conversations, and even in moments of decision-making. "This flame is not just a symbol," Master Soryu reminded them. "It is a mirror of your inner state. Learn to live with it, and you will learn to live at the pace of love."

Over the weeks that followed, the students discovered profound changes. Kael learned to temper his impulsiveness, finding joy in deliberate actions. He began to pause during conversations, ensuring his words reflected care and thoughtfulness. Amara overcame her fear of failure, embracing a confident steadiness. She realized hesitation dimmed her light, and instead, she began to act with quiet determination. Jorin, who had always been mindful, deepened his awareness of how the flame extended into every corner of life, even in the smallest interactions.

Conclusion and Reflection

The lesson of the flame transformed not only the students but also those around them. Their newfound way of living inspired others in the community. People noticed how their interactions felt more meaningful, as though touched by a deeper light.

Master Soryu's wisdom echoed in their hearts: "The flame within you is love's gentle light. Let it guide your every step, not in haste or hesitation, but with the steady rhythm of a heart aligned with compassion."

Questions for Reflection

1. When do you feel rushed or slowed by external pressures? How does this affect your inner flame?
2. How can you bring mindfulness to your speech, actions, and relationships?
3. What steps can you take to ensure you are living at the pace of love, kindness, or cooperation?
4. How might your interactions change if you honored the pace of your inner flame?

Dancing Buddha's Quote

"The flame within you is love's gentle light. Let it guide your every step, not in haste or hesitation, but with the steady rhythm of a heart aligned with compassion."

Gregory K. Cadotte

STORY 35 – THE FINAL STEP

Introduction: The Pilgrimage Begins

The morning sun rose over the mountain, painting the sky in soft hues of gold and pink. The monk and his three students—Arun, Sita, and Meena—stood at the base of the winding path that would lead them to the temple perched high above. The journey was said to be both grueling and transformative, with steep inclines, rocky terrain, and unexpected challenges.

"Master," Meena said, adjusting her pack, "why do we need to climb to the temple? Can't we meditate and find wisdom where we are?"

The monk smiled, his expression calm. "The journey to the temple is not about reaching the summit, Meena. It is about the steps we take along the way. Today, we will learn that the final step is not the end—it is the beginning."

The students exchanged uncertain glances but followed the monk as he began the ascent, his staff tapping steadily against the stones.

Section 1: The Weight of the Pack

The path was narrow and steep, bordered by towering pines that swayed gently in the cool breeze. The students moved in single file, their packs heavy with provisions. As the trail grew steeper, Arun began to lag behind, his face tight with effort.

"Master," Arun called, his voice strained, "this pack is too heavy. Why must we carry so much?"

The monk paused, turning to face his student. "What do you carry, Arun?" he asked.

"Food, water, supplies," Arun replied. "Everything we need for the journey."

"And what else?" the monk pressed gently. "Do you carry worries, fears, or doubts?"

Arun hesitated, then nodded. "Yes, Master. I carry those too."

The monk gestured for Arun to remove his pack and sit. "Take a moment to reflect," he said. "The weight of the journey is not in the path but in what we carry. To reach the final step, we must first release what weighs us down."

Arun closed his eyes and breathed deeply. As he imagined setting aside his fears and doubts, his body seemed to lighten.

The monk added softly, "You might begin to notice... how much lighter each step feels when you let go of just one thing."

When Arun stood again, his steps felt surer, his pack less burdensome. The gentle breeze seemed to whisper encouragement, carrying away what he had left behind.

Section 2: The False Summit

After a brief rest, the group continued upward. The trail curved sharply, and a clearing revealed what seemed to be the temple, its golden roof glinting in the sunlight.

"There it is!" Sita exclaimed, quickening her pace. "We're almost there!"

But as they reached the clearing, they saw the truth. The temple was still far above, the path continuing to climb into the clouds. Sita's shoulders sagged, and frustration clouded her face.

"Why does it feel like we'll never reach the top?" she asked.

The monk knelt and picked up a small stone, holding it in his palm. "This stone," he said, "is like our focus on the final step. When we fixate on the end, we miss the beauty of the journey. The false summit reminds us to be present, for each step carries its own wisdom."

Sita took the stone and held it tightly. As she walked, she began to notice the sound of birdsong, the rustle of leaves in the wind, and the warmth of the sun on her skin. Each step felt less like a struggle and more like a gift.

The monk's voice echoed gently, "And perhaps you'll discover... the summit is not just above but also within."

Section 3: Guided Meditation: Walking Each Step

The monk led his students to a quiet grove where the sound of a trickling stream offered a sense of calm. He gestured for them to sit and close their eyes.

"Let us meditate on the steps we take," he said, his voice a steady rhythm.

"Close your eyes and take a deep breath. Feel the earth beneath you, strong and supportive."

"Imagine yourself walking the path to the temple. With each step, notice the texture of the ground beneath your feet—the coolness of the stones, the softness of the earth."

"Now, picture a pack on your back. It feels heavy, but as you walk, you begin to open it. One by one, you remove the items that weigh you down—doubts, fears, expectations. Feel the weight lighten."

"With each step, you focus on the present. The sound of the wind, the warmth of the sun, the rhythm of your breath. Say silently to yourself: 'Each step is whole. Each step is enough.'"

"As you near the temple, realize the final step is not the goal but a continuation of all the steps before it. Feel the joy of the journey, the freedom of the release."

The students sat quietly, their breathing deep and steady, as the meditation unfolded. The grove seemed to hum with the energy of their stillness.

The monk added softly, "And as you release, you might find yourself wondering... what other weights could you set down today?"

Section 4: The Final Step

As the group neared the summit, the temple came into full view, its intricate carvings glowing in the golden light of the setting sun. The students stood at the base of the final staircase, their faces alight with both relief and awe.

"Master," Meena said, "we are finally here."

The monk nodded, his voice warm. "Yes, Meena. But tell me, what have you learned along the way?"

"I learned that the weight I carried was not just physical," Arun said. "When I let go of my fears, the journey felt lighter."

Sita added, "I learned to appreciate each moment, even the hard ones. The false summit taught me to see the beauty in the steps, not just the destination."

Meena smiled. "And I learned that the journey itself is the temple. Each step we took was part of the final step."

The monk's expression grew radiant. "The final step is not the end, my students. It is the culmination of every step before it, and the beginning of every step to come. When we live fully in each moment, we realize that we are already whole, already complete."

With that, the group ascended the final stairs together, their hearts light and their spirits full. The temple doors welcomed them with an unspoken truth: they had always been enough.

Affirmations

"Each step I take is whole and complete in itself."

"I release what weighs me down and embrace the freedom of the journey."

Conclusion: The Journey Continues

As the students stood within the temple, they felt a profound stillness settle over them. The journey had tested their strength, patience, and perspective, but it had also revealed their inner wholeness. The monk looked at each of them, his eyes filled with quiet pride.

"The path to the temple is the same as the path within," he said. "Each step, each moment, each breath—these are the pieces of wholeness we often overlook. The final step is not a destination but a reminder of the journey's truth."

The students bowed deeply, their hearts open and at peace. As the sun dipped below the horizon, the temple seemed to glow with the light of their understanding.

Questions for Reflection

1. What are you carrying in your "pack" that may be weighing you down?
2. When have you fixated on a goal and missed the beauty of the steps leading to it?
3. How can you release judgment and embrace the present step as complete in itself?
4. What moments in your life felt like false summits, and how did they help you grow?
5. How can you cultivate the awareness that each step of your journey is whole in itself?
6.

Dancing Buddha Quote

"The final step is not the end of the journey but the realization that each step is whole in itself."

PART FIVE

Wholeness

PART FIVE

WHOLENESS – UNITY AND THE DANCING BUDDHA

The Dancing Buddha: Embracing Wholeness

The Dancing Buddha is a symbol of joyful completeness, a figure that moves with grace yet stands firmly grounded. It invites us to embrace the flow of life while remaining centered, to celebrate the contrasts within us—the light and the shadow, the movement and the stillness, the moments of clarity and those of confusion. In this final section, we explore the idea of wholeness, where the integration of all aspects of ourselves leads to a sense of unity and inner harmony.

The Dance of Life: Flowing with Wholeness

Think of the sky. It is vast and infinite, holding space for the sun, the clouds, and the stars. The sky does not reject the storm, nor does it cling to the sunshine. It allows all to pass through, knowing that each moment is part of the greater whole. And just as the sky embraces all that arises, you can begin to allow yourself to fully experience each part of your journey.

Imagine yourself on a dance floor. The music begins, unpredictable yet inviting. At first, you hesitate, uncertain of the rhythm. But as you relax into the movement, something shifts. You feel the tempo, the flow, and suddenly, you are not just moving; you are dancing. And in this dance, there is no "right" step, no "wrong" step—only presence, only movement, only this moment.

As you picture this, you may notice a sense of ease growing within you, a knowing that life itself is this dance. That each step, each pause, each turn brings you deeper into the rhythm of your own unfolding. And with each breath, you find yourself feeling more connected, more present, more whole.

Beyond Dualities: Dissolving Illusions

At the heart of wholeness is the realization that duality is only a frame of reference, not a fundamental truth. We often perceive life through opposites—light and dark, good and bad, strength and vulnerability—but these are not separate forces. They are simply different vantage points along the same journey. And as you begin to explore this idea, you may find that the distinctions between "opposites" become softer, more fluid, more like a dance between perspectives.

For a moment, allow yourself to step outside of these contrasts. Imagine viewing your life not as a series of opposites, but as a continuum, a seamless flow. Notice what happens when you release the need to categorize each experience as one thing or another. Does the struggle become simply another movement of growth? Does the darkness become the place where light is discovered?

As you continue to reflect, you may notice how comforting it is to realize that no single experience defines you. That who you are is far greater, far vaster than any single moment. And as this awareness settles within you, you might even find a sense of freedom, a sense of peace in knowing that you do not need to "fix" anything. That you are already whole.

Integration: The Path to Inner Harmony

Integration is the process of weaving together all the lessons, experiences, and truths you have gathered on your journey. It is not about fixing or solving but about bringing everything into alignment—mind, body, heart, and spirit. And right now, you might even begin to feel that alignment growing within you, as if each piece of your journey is gently finding its place.

Imagine a stained-glass window. Each fragment of glass is unique, some clear, some colorful, some seemingly out of place when viewed alone. But when light shines through, a breathtaking image is revealed. Your life is much the same. Each moment, each experience, whether joyful or challenging, is part of the masterpiece you are creating. And with each breath, you may find yourself stepping back, seeing the full picture more clearly, and realizing just how beautiful it truly is.

The Gift of Wholeness: Remembering Who You Are

Wholeness is not something you achieve; it is something you remember. It is the realization that you were never truly broken, only in the process of becoming. And the more you relax into this truth, the more you may notice a gentle sense of ease, as if something inside you is sighing in relief.

The Dancing Buddha shows us that wholeness is not a destination but a way of being. It is found in the present moment, in the willingness to embrace life as it is, and in the courage to love ourselves fully. And perhaps, as you reflect on this, you can feel that love growing within you now, in a way that feels both familiar and new at the same time.

As you move through the stories and meditations in this section, allow yourself to feel, sense, and imagine. Let yourself be the sky, vast and accepting. Let yourself be the dancer, fluid and alive. And let yourself be the Buddha, grounded and joyful in the wholeness of your being.

Affirmations for Wholeness

- *I honor every part of my journey, knowing it has shaped me into who I am today.*
- *I embrace the dance of life, finding balance and beauty in all its rhythms.*
- *I trust the unfolding of my path, knowing that I am already whole.*

These affirmations can serve as gentle reminders as you move forward, helping you integrate the lessons of this section into your daily life. And as you take a breath now, you may notice a quiet sense of knowing deep inside you—that the path to wholeness is not about becoming someone new, but about remembering the fullness of who you have always been.

Let us step into the dance together.

Gregory K. Cadotte

STORY 36 – THE METHOD ACTOR

A Unique Beginning

The old Volkswagen van sputtered and coughed as it climbed the winding road to the Hollywood Hills. Its faded paint, a patchwork of turquoise and rust, gleamed dully under the California sun. Inside, Master Tao sat serenely in the passenger seat, while Mira clutched the wheel with determination. Aiko, sprawled on the backseat surrounded by empty snack wrappers, hummed to herself, while Ravi scrolled through a digital map, frowning.

"Are we even going the right way?" Ravi asked, peering out the window at the winding road.

Master Tao smiled. "And as you wonder about that now, perhaps you can already begin to notice... that sometimes, the right way is simply the way we are on."

The students groaned collectively. They had grown used to Master Tao's cryptic wisdom, but his timing always seemed a little too perfect—or infuriating, depending on the moment.

Ahead, the Hollywood Sign came into view, its giant white letters perched against the scrubby hillside like a beacon of dreams. Mira's grip on the wheel tightened slightly, a flicker of something unspoken in her eyes.

Master Tao raised a hand, signaling Mira to pull over into a dusty overlook.

"Why here?" Aiko asked, hopping out of the van.

"Because," Master Tao said, gesturing toward the iconic sign, "this is where the lesson begins."

Mira exhaled slowly, as if she had been holding something inside for far too long.

The Hollywood Sign and the Actor's Role

The students gathered around Master Tao, the city sprawling in a smoggy haze far below them. He gestured toward the Hollywood Sign, his voice calm but charged with curiosity.

"What does this sign mean to you?"

Aiko squinted. "It's... Hollywood. Movies. Fame."

"An illusion," Ravi muttered. "It's just a facade—a sign pretending to be more than it is."

Mira, quiet as ever, tilted her head. "Maybe it's a symbol. It makes people dream." Her voice carried a note of something deeper, something personal.

Master Tao nodded. "And as you listen now, you may already start to sense... that everything plays a role in this great performance."

He glanced at Mira, his gaze knowing. "Some roles we choose.

Some, we inherit. And some, we resist."

Mira swallowed hard, looking away. Ravi and Aiko exchanged a glance but said nothing.

"To understand the sign," Master Tao continued, "you must first understand the actor behind it. And to understand the actor, you must see the energy that gives it life. Let us explore."

The Beat-Up Van and the Divine Method Actor

Back in the van, Master Tao directed Mira to an old park near a forgotten part of the hills. They pulled into a dirt lot where weeds pushed through cracked asphalt. A small amphitheater lay abandoned, its wooden stage bleached gray by the sun.

"What are we doing here?" Ravi asked, stepping out cautiously.

"This place is like the sign," Master Tao said. "It once held life, a story. Now it's empty, yet its essence lingers."

He climbed onto the stage with surprising agility and turned to face his students. "The Divine is like a method actor. It inhabits every role fully—every leaf, every animal, every person, every sign. The script may change, but the energy behind it remains."

Mira hesitated at the edge of the stage. "But what if a role isn't meant for you?"

Master Tao's smile was soft. "Ah. Is it the role… or the way you are playing it?"

Aiko touched Mira's arm lightly. "Maybe you don't have to act… maybe you just have to be."

Mira let out a breath she hadn't realized she was holding. She stepped forward.

Guided Meditation: Seeing the Actor Within

Master Tao gestured for the students to sit on the old amphitheater seats, the warm wood creaking under their weight. The setting sun bathed the space in golden light, and the Hollywood Sign gleamed faintly in the distance.

"Close your eyes," he said.

"And as you do, you might start to feel… the sense of being here now, more fully."

"Imagine yourself as an actor on a stage. Around you are props: a tree, a stone, a car, the wind. Notice how each of these has its own presence, its own energy. And perhaps, as you observe this, you can begin to sense something deeper."

A pause.

"Now, picture yourself playing a role—the character of you. Your name, your history, your personality—all carefully crafted like lines in a script. And notice what happens as you step back… as you observe yourself, the actor, playing this role so perfectly."

Mira's breathing deepened. The tension in her shoulders softened.

"And as you do, you may begin to sense… that all of this is connected. That the stage, the roles, the props, the script… are all part of a greater performance."

The students' breathing slowed. Aiko's face softened with wonder. Ravi's frown disappeared, replaced by a look of contemplation. Mira's expression turned peaceful, her head tilting slightly as if listening to something distant.

Master Tao's voice softened further.

"And when the curtain falls, the actor does not vanish… it simply steps into the wings, waiting for its next role."

A single tear slid down Mira's cheek, but she was smiling.

Conclusion

Back at the temple, the students gathered under the stars, the van parked in its usual spot, now seeming less ordinary.

Master Tao spoke softly.

"And maybe, as you move through your life, you will begin to notice... the roles you play, the scenes that unfold... and the quiet presence behind it all."

Mira exhaled, a weight lifting.

"Maybe," she whispered. And this time, she believed it.

The students bowed deeply, their hearts filled with wonder at the thought of the infinite energy playing out its roles.

Affirmations

"I recognize the Divine energy in all things, acting with purpose and grace."

"I trust the cycles of life, knowing that nothing is truly lost—only transformed."

Questions for Reflection

1. How does thinking of the world as a divine performance change your view of life?
2. Can you see the energy behind the "roles" in your own life and surroundings?

3. How can this understanding help you embrace change or loss?
4. What role are you currently playing in life? How does it serve the greater whole?
5. If the energy behind all things is one, how does that shift your relationships with others?

Dancing Buddha's Quote

"The actor plays the role until the curtain falls, but the energy behind the mask never fades. See the Divine in every performance, and you will never lose sight of the eternal."

STORY 37 – THE STATIC PRESENT

Introduction: The Flow of Time and Stillness of Now

In the heart of Kyoto, where cherry blossoms danced in the wind, a temple stood on the banks of the Kamo River. The air carried the scent of incense, and the rhythmic chirping of cicadas blended with the soft murmur of water against stone. The temple, made of rich cedar and adorned with golden accents, had stood for centuries, watching the world change around it.

Inside the temple gardens, beneath the dappled shade of an ancient maple tree, a monk sat with his students—Ren, Aiko, and Satoshi. The sky was painted in hues of rose and amber, marking the slow descent of the sun. A cool breeze rustled the leaves, sending delicate petals drifting through the air.

"Today," the monk said, his voice like the gentle whisper of wind through bamboo, "we will dissolve the illusion of time."

Ren frowned, adjusting his glasses. "Master, how can we dissolve something that governs our every moment? Clocks move, the seasons change, people grow old."

The monk's smile was serene. "You believe time moves, but it does not. You move. And by the end of today, you will see that time is neither your enemy nor your master—it is an illusion."

Part 1: The Illusion of Motion

The monk traced a circle in the sand with his finger, slow and deliberate. "Picture this: The present moment is not something slipping away. It is eternal, always here. What we call time is simply the shifting of shadows and the movement of bodies."

He pointed toward the river. "Look at the water. It flows, yet if you stand still, you will see that the river itself does not move. The water moves within it. The present is like the riverbed—stable, holding space for all movement. The flow of water, the movement of days, is not time slipping away, but the movement of form within stillness."

He gestured toward the sun, dipping toward the horizon. "Now, imagine the Earth. It spins, it moves around the sun, but it never leaves the present moment. From the vastness of space, there is no past or future—only the eternal now in which the Earth travels. You are like the Earth, always in the present, never outside of it."

The monk's voice softened, carrying a hypnotic rhythm. "And as you hear these words, you may begin to notice awareness deepening… a sense of stillness, a realization that you have never truly left this moment."

Aiko tilted her head. "But Master, if time is an illusion, why do we feel it pressing upon us?"

"Because you measure yourself against movement," the monk replied. "You feel rushed not because time moves, but because you believe you must keep up. The truth is, you are already here. You have never left. And as you accept this truth, you may find yourself breathing more easily, feeling lighter, more present."

Part 2: The Gravity of Existence

The monk picked up a fallen petal and let it drift onto his palm. "Tell me, why does this petal fall?"

Satoshi shrugged. "Gravity?"

"Exactly. And yet, do you blame time for this petal's descent? No, you accept that gravity is at work. In the same way, aging, change, growth—they are not caused by time, but by forces within the universe. It is not time that pulls you forward, but gravity that holds you down. Strengthen your body, sharpen your mind, and you will experience time differently—not as something slipping away, but as something you move within."

The monk's voice took on a rhythmic cadence, drawing the students deeper into contemplation. "And as you think about this now, you may notice something else—how easy it is to release the pressure of time, how effortlessly you step into the present moment."

Ren's eyes widened. "So we don't run out of time—we run out of strength?"

The monk nodded. "And when you realize this, you can begin to feel a new sense of control over your life. When you stop waiting for time to carry you, you understand that it never was. Time does not act upon you; you act within it."

Part 3: Time Does Not Change Anything

The monk stood, motioning for the students to follow him toward the temple's stone path. They walked in silence, their feet pressing softly against the earth. A koi pond stretched before them, its surface smooth except for the occasional ripple from the swimming fish.

The monk gestured to the water. "Does this pond change with time?"

Aiko hesitated. "Yes, Master. The water moves, the fish grow."

"No," the monk said gently. "The pond does not change because of time. It changes because of the movement within it. The wind stirs the surface, the fish swim, the rain falls—but time does nothing. If nothing moved, the pond would remain exactly as it is."

He looked at each student in turn, his voice now softer, guiding. "And as you begin to see this truth, you may find yourself letting go of the idea that time is responsible for change… and instead, you may begin to notice the power you've always had."

Ren exhaled slowly. "So all this time, I thought I was waiting for time to fix things. But really, I just wasn't doing anything."

The monk nodded. "And now, as you realize this, you may already feel new possibilities opening before you."

Part 4: Meditation on Stillness

The monk led them to the river's edge, where a wooden deck stretched over the water. The gentle ripples reflected the golden sky, a canvas of ever-shifting light.

"Sit," he instructed, his voice soft but firm. "Close your eyes."

The students obeyed, the sounds of nature wrapping around them.

"Imagine yourself standing in an open field," the monk began, his voice weaving through their thoughts. "The field stretches infinitely, beyond sight, beyond the horizon. This field is the present moment—vast, endless, still."

A breeze caressed their skin. "And as you breathe in, you may notice how easy it is to settle into this awareness, how time dissolves the more you focus on this space."

Aiko's breath deepened. She could feel the weight of time dissolve, replaced by a quiet, powerful stillness.

"You are not running out of time," the monk continued. "You are here. You have always been here."

Affirmations

"I am fully present in this moment, embracing the infinite now."

"Change does not come with time; it comes with action, and I am ready to act."

Questions for Further Discussion

1. Have you ever felt like time was running out? How does this lesson change your perspective?
2. How does understanding that gravity—not time—is the true force of change shift your mindset?

3. What areas of your life could transform if you stopped waiting for time to make a difference and instead took action now?
4. How can you practice being more present in your daily routine?

Dancing Buddha's Quote

"You are not running out of time. Nothing changes because of time. Nothing will change until you change it. Like the Earth moving through space, you are never ahead, never behind... only ever here."

STORY 38 – THE ONENESS OF BEING

The Gathering of Students

In a worn-out city, where the streets were cracked and crumbling, there stood an ancient monastery. The structure had weathered time and wear, much like the city itself. The roof sagged under years of neglect, but its walls, carved from stone, stood firm, sheltering the teachings of a long-forgotten wisdom. It was here that Master Khenpo, a monk of great renown, imparted his knowledge to his three devoted students.

Master Khenpo was a man of few words but great presence. His eyes, soft yet piercing, reflected a depth of understanding that could only come from years of meditation and self-reflection. His students—Tenzin, Dorje, and Lhamo—were young, eager, and each sought enlightenment in their own way. Tenzin was thoughtful and quiet, Dorje fiery and passionate, and Lhamo full of curiosity and energy.

One crisp morning, with the city's distant hum barely reaching the monastery, Master Khenpo gathered his students in the courtyard. The scent of old wood and incense mingled with the earthy smell of the soil beneath their feet. The monastery grounds were surrounded by rows of corn stalks, their leaves rustling gently in the wind. The small garden was tended to by the monks, and it seemed to thrive in the otherwise decaying city.

The students sat on the ground, their legs crossed, their eyes fixed on their teacher. Master Khenpo stood before them, his robes flowing like water, and he began speaking, his voice calm and steady.

The Teachings of Unity

"Today, we will talk about the nature of consciousness," Master Khenpo began, his voice calm and steady. "You may see yourselves as separate individuals, but this is an illusion. You are always connected, and with each breath, you are beginning to realize this connection more clearly. You have always been part of the whole, and with each passing moment, you are more deeply aware of this truth."

He paused, allowing the students a moment to reflect. "Let's think about the beginning of life itself. In the beginning, there was a single cell, and when it divided, it did not become two separate beings. It remained the same being, simply expressed in two places. With each division, that same essence, that same consciousness, simply spread outward, moving through many forms—but it was never separate."

Master Khenpo let the students absorb this idea before continuing. "You see, when a cell divides, it does not create something new—it simply continues to express the same essence in two places. And with each division, it grows, but it remains one. As you breathe now, you are reminded that you too are part of this flow. The essence of you has never been separate from the whole. It simply expresses itself in many forms, and you are a part of it, always."

Tenzin's brow furrowed. "Master, how can this single cell still be one if it is split and multiplied?"

Master Khenpo smiled gently. "Imagine this: the flame from one candle lights another. The second flame isn't separate from the first. It is the same fire, carried forward. The fire is still one, even though it appears in different places. The same is true for consciousness. As it divides, it never becomes separate—it simply continues the original awareness, expressing itself in infinite forms."

Lhamo's eyes sparkled with understanding. "So, like the cell, we are all part of the same consciousness, always expressing ourselves in new ways, but never separate."

"Exactly," Master Khenpo nodded. "Every thought, every feeling, every person, every experience is part of the same consciousness. And as you breathe, you can feel this connection more deeply. You may not always notice it, but it is always there, within you and around you, growing, expanding, just like that first cell."

The Struggle of Perception

Dorje, his mind full of questions, leaned forward. "But Master, if we are all one, why does the world seem so divided? Why do we fight? Why do we feel separate?"

Master Khenpo's gaze softened as he looked at Dorje. "The

world is not divided, but differentiated. Consciousness takes on countless forms, not to become separate, but to know itself more fully. The corn in the field and the dog barking—they are not other than you. They are you, in a different place, carrying the same life forward."

Dorje's brow remained furrowed. "But if that's true, why don't we feel it? Why do people suffer from loneliness? Why do we look at others and feel different?"

Master Khenpo inhaled slowly, then spoke with the kind of patience that comes from seeing beyond illusion.

"We do not feel oneness because we are born into forgetfulness. From the moment we enter this world, we awaken to a story already being told. We are given a name. We are told who we are, where we belong, and how we are different from others. And in this way, a great illusion takes hold.

Because our bodies are different, we believe we must be separate. Because our experiences vary, we believe we must be alone in them. And because we see the world through these individual perspectives, we begin to fashion stories of separation. Stories that say: 'I am here, and you are there. I am me, and you are other.'"

Dorje exhaled, his hands resting on his knees. "And once we believe those stories... we act as if they're real."

Master Khenpo nodded. "Yes. We begin to see division where there is only difference. We believe we must prove ourselves, defend ourselves, or stand apart. We chase belonging in groups, in identities, in roles—because deep down, we feel the loss of something we do not remember. We do not realize that the very thing we are seeking—connection, unity, home—was never lost. It was only forgotten."

Lhamo's expression was full of wonder. "So, we are all like dreamers who forgot we were dreaming?"

Master Khenpo smiled. "Exactly. And the journey of life is

the slow waking from that dream. The suffering, the searching, the longing—all of it is the movement back toward remembrance. And when we remember, even for a moment, the illusion begins to dissolve."

Tenzin, who had been quiet, finally spoke. "But what if someone never remembers? What if they spend their whole life lost in the illusion?"

Master Khenpo's gaze did not waver. "No one is truly lost, Tenzin. Some take longer. Some resist. Some must struggle against their own reflection before they recognize it as their own. But just as every wave must return to the ocean, every being must return to itself."

A hush settled over the students, a stillness that was not empty but full—as if something sacred had just been understood, even if it could not yet be put into words.

Master Khenpo's voice was quieter now, almost a whisper.

"You have never been separate. Not in this breath. Not in the next. The only difference is whether you remember."

Understanding Oneness

Master Khenpo's voice softened further, and he spoke as if guiding the students into a deeper state of awareness. "With each passing moment, you are becoming more attuned to the oneness that is always present. Each breath you take brings you closer to the realization that you are part of everything around you. You may begin to notice, even now, that as you sit here, you are already experiencing this connection. Each exhale is an expansion of awareness, allowing you to feel more deeply that you are not separate, but one."

The Journey Through the City

Later that afternoon, Master Khenpo led his students on a walk through the city. The air was cool, and the bustling of the streets felt distant as the students walked in silence. The city seemed less fragmented now, as they passed by people working, children laughing, and vendors calling out.

"Remember," Master Khenpo said, "everything you encounter is part of the same flow, the same consciousness. Even as you walk through this city, you are connected to everything around you. The people you meet, the sounds you hear—they are not separate from you. They are part of you, part of the flow of life."

They reached a market where a vendor offered them fresh bread. Master Khenpo accepted and handed a piece to Lhamo. "This bread," he said, "is no different from the air you breathe, from the earth that nourished it, or from you. It is all part of the same movement, the same flow, taking many forms, yet remaining one."

Guided Meditation Scene

That evening, Master Khenpo gathered the students in the meditation hall. The room was lit by the soft flicker of oil lamps, their light dancing on the ancient stone walls. The students sat in a circle, their postures upright, their hands resting gently on their knees. Master Khenpo guided them into meditation, his voice steady and calming.

"Close your eyes, and take a deep breath. Feel the air moving in and out of your body, flowing effortlessly. As you breathe, feel yourself becoming more connected, more attuned to the oneness that exists around you. Each breath brings you closer to the truth that you are not separate from the world."

"Now, imagine a single point of light at the center of your chest. This light is the essence of who you are—whole, complete, and connected. With each breath, see this light expand outward. It grows, filling your body, radiating into the space around you. You are not separate. You are part of this light, and this light is part of you. As you breathe, you feel this connection grow stronger, deepening with every breath."

The students sat quietly, their faces serene, their breathing slow and deep. The room seemed to hum with a silent energy, a shared understanding that the truth of oneness was already within them, waiting to be recognized.

Returning Home: The Affirmation of Oneness

As the sun began to set, casting a golden glow over the cornfields, the students walked silently back to the monastery. The evening air was cool, and the distant sound of crickets added a rhythm to their steps.

Master Khenpo turned to them, his voice warm and steady. "You are already beginning to see the truth more clearly. With each breath, you are becoming more deeply aware of your oneness. This journey has only just begun, and each day, you will find yourself more connected, more attuned to the world around you."

Affirmations

"I am a unique expression of the infinite oneness, connected to all that exists."

"Through every experience, I remember the truth: I am not separate; I am whole."

Questions for Further Consideration

1. How does the idea that a single consciousness differentiates into many forms change how you view yourself and others?
2. What practical steps can you take to experience oneness in your daily life?
3. How do feelings of separateness arise in your life, and how might meditation or reflection help to bridge this gap?
4. What lessons can you draw from the metaphor of a single cell dividing without becoming separate?
5. How can you carry the awareness of oneness into moments of conflict or misunderstanding?

Dancing Buddha's Quote

"The universe does not divide itself to understand itself; it expands itself. In this expansion, every star, every breath, every moment is one."

STORY 39 – THE INFINITE WHOLE

Introduction

The monastery sat perched on a cliff overlooking an endless valley. It was a place where silence spoke louder than words, where the whispers of the wind carried truths, and where Master Samaya guided his three students—Nalin, Priya, and Kavi—toward a profound understanding of existence.

One evening, as the sun dipped below the horizon, painting the sky in hues of amber and rose, Nalin sat with his master beneath a gnarled, ancient tree. His brows furrowed in thought, he turned to the monk.

"Master," he asked, "why do I feel so small in this vast

universe? I am but a speck of dust in an endless cosmos."

Samaya gazed at the horizon, the golden light dancing in his eyes. He picked up a fallen leaf, its edges curled and veins like rivers on a map.

"Do you see this leaf, Nalin? Tell me, which is greater: the leaf or the tree it fell from?"

Nalin frowned, confused. "The tree, of course. The leaf is but a part of it."

Samaya smiled gently. "And yet, the tree would not be complete without its leaves. Each leaf carries the essence of the tree within it. Now tell me, which is greater: the body or the toe?"

Nalin chuckled, thinking it a simple question. "The body, of course. The toe is just a small part of the whole."

Samaya leaned closer, his voice soft and knowing. "Is it? The body is not whole without the toe, just as the toe is not whole without the body. They are two expressions of the same oneness, each carrying the other. The toe holds the body, and the body holds the toe. Do you see?"

Nalin's laughter faded, replaced by a thoughtful silence.

Priya, observing from a distance, murmured, "Master, if all things are part of a whole, how can we feel so separate?"

Samaya nodded, a glimmer of approval in his eyes. "Let us continue, and perhaps the answer will reveal itself."

The River and the Drop

The next morning, Samaya led his students to a river. The water was clear and cool, rushing over smooth stones. He cupped his hands, filling them with water, and held them out to Nalin.

"Look at this water," Samaya said. "Is it separate from the river?"

Nalin tilted his head, puzzled. "Yes, Master. You've taken it from the river."

Samaya let the water trickle through his fingers and back into the stream. "And now?"

Nalin hesitated. "Now it is part of the river again."

Samaya smiled. "It was never separate, Nalin. Even when held in my hands, it remained the river. The drop contains the river's essence, and the river contains countless drops. They are not two but one, flowing into and out of each other."

Kavi, watching closely, asked, "But Master, how does this help us in our struggles? Knowing we are drops in a river does not ease the burden of daily life."

Samaya's gaze softened. "Because when you see yourself as the river, not just the drop, burdens flow rather than weigh. You realize you are supported by something greater, and in that, you find peace."

Nalin crouched by the water's edge, letting it rush over his fingers. "So, we are like the drops, Master? Part of a greater whole?"

"Exactly," Samaya said. "And yet, the whole is within us as well. You are the universe expressing itself as Nalin, just as the river expresses itself as this drop. There is no greater or lesser, only one infinite dance."

The Breath of the Cosmos

That afternoon, as they walked back toward the monastery, Samaya gestured toward the sky.

"Nalin, take a deep breath."

Nalin inhaled slowly, feeling the cool air enter his lungs.

"Now exhale."

As he released the breath, Samaya continued, "That air was never yours. It was borrowed. A moment ago, it belonged to the trees, to the mountains, to the ocean. Before that, it passed through countless others—through creatures, through rivers, through centuries of life before you."

Nalin's eyes widened.

"The air does not belong to you, yet you depend on it. The water does not belong to you, yet it flows through you. The matter in your bones, your skin, your blood—none of it is truly yours. It has been here long before you and will continue long after."

Samaya's voice deepened, as if carrying the weight of a thousand years.

"You are not separate from the world. You are an intersection of powerful cycles. Water moves through you, only to return to the rivers and clouds. Air passes through you, only to dance with the wind once more. Matter enters and leaves you, returning to the earth from which it came. You are not a fixed thing, but a momentary meeting place for the movement of life itself."

Priya's voice was barely above a whisper. "Then we are not isolated beings at all."

Samaya nodded. "You are the breath of the cosmos, the movement of the earth, the flowing of rivers. You are the infinite passing through this moment."

Guided Meditation: The Universe Within

That evening, as the stars emerged one by one, Samaya guided his students through a meditation.

"Close your eyes," he said, his voice calm and steady.

"Feel the rhythm of your breath. With each inhale, draw in

the vastness of the universe. With each exhale, let yourself flow back into it. The air you breathe has passed through a thousand generations. The water in your body has been part of storms and seas, of mountains and rivers. The matter that forms you was once the planet itself. You are not apart from these things; they move through you as you move through them."

A pause. The silence deepened.

"Now, feel your heartbeat. Each pulse mirrors the rhythm of the stars, the waves, the turning of the earth. You are not separate from these things. They are you, and you are them. Breathe, feel, and know: the universe is within you, and you are within it."

The students sat in silence, their breaths synchronized with the hum of the night, a profound peace settling over them.

The Dance of Oneness

Days turned into weeks, and Nalin began to see the interconnectedness of all things. He marveled at the way bees danced among the flowers, carrying life from one to the other. He saw how the rain nourished the earth, which in turn gave rise to the trees that provided shade and shelter. He felt the pulse of life in his own veins and knew it mirrored the rhythm of the cosmos.

One day, as they sat by the river, Nalin turned to Samaya and said, "Master, I see it now. The body and the toe, the drop and the river, the breath and the wind—they are all the same. The universe breathes through us as we breathe through it. We are its expression, and it is ours."

Samaya's smile was radiant, as if the stars themselves shone in his eyes. "Yes, Nalin. There is no small or great, no separate or whole. There is only one infinite being, endlessly loving, endlessly expressing. To live is to dance within this oneness, to love is to feel its embrace. And to know this is to be free."

As the first light of dawn broke over the valley, Nalin felt it rise within him, a flame of oneness ignited by the infinite whole. He smiled, knowing he would never feel small again.

Affirmations

"I am the universe expressing itself; I am whole and connected."

"In every breath, I feel the infinite within and around me."

Questions for Further Reflection

1. If air, water, and matter are constantly flowing through you, can you truly call your body "yours"? How does this realization shift your sense of identity?
2. In what ways do you feel separate from the world around you? How might seeing yourself as an intersection of natural cycles change your perspective?
3. How does recognizing that you are the breath of the cosmos, the movement of the earth, and the flow of rivers affect the way you live?
4. Think of a moment when you felt deeply connected to something greater—perhaps in nature, in silence, or in stillness. What was different in that moment?
5. How does understanding yourself as a temporary intersection of powerful cycles impact the way you approach life, death, and change?

6. What practices could help you remember your connection to the infinite when daily life makes you feel small or isolated?

Dancing Buddha's Quote

"You are the dance and the dancer, the song and the silence. The infinite whole moves through you, and you move through it."

Gregory K. Cadotte

STORY 40 - THE RIVER OF CONSCIOUSNESS

Introduction

In a quiet temple high above the cliffs of Bhutan, where the wind carried the scent of cedar and the prayer flags danced against the sky, Master Rohan sat with his students. He was an old monk, his saffron robes faded from years beneath the sun. Before him, a small group of seekers sat cross-legged, eyes filled with questions they had not yet found the words to ask.

"Today," he began, his voice smooth like water over stone, "we will take a journey—not across mountains or through forests, but within. A journey beyond the names you were given, beyond the faces you wear. A journey into the vastness of who you truly are."

He smiled gently. "Are you ready?"

A hush fell over the group. A young woman named Mira

nodded first. Then Ravi, then Jian, then the others, until all sat in expectant silence.

"Then close your eyes," the monk whispered. "And let us begin."

Section One: The River of Time

"Imagine yourself standing by a river," Master Rohan's voice was a steady guide, rich with imagery that settled into the students' minds. "The water moves effortlessly, carrying leaves, twigs, reflections of clouds. Each ripple, a moment passing. Each current, a story you have told yourself."

A deep breath. A long pause.

"Look closer," he continued, his tone softening, aligning with their breathing. "There—your childhood. A younger version of you laughing, crying, playing. Further down the stream—your fears, your triumphs, the roles you have played. Watch them flow past. No need to hold on. Just observe. Just let go... and as you do, notice how much lighter you feel."

Ravi swallowed. He saw himself at eight years old, clutching his father's hand before he let go forever. He exhaled, watching the scene drift downstream.

"And as you step back from the river's edge, feeling the warmth of the sun on your skin, the cool breeze against your face, you notice something... you are no longer caught in the current. The stories are not you. You are the one watching. And because you can watch, you can choose how to feel. And you might just find, in this moment, a deep sense of peace."

Section Two: The Infinite Sky

"Let your awareness rise now," Master Rohan instructed. "Look up. The sky is endless, stretching beyond sight. Clouds move across it—just as thoughts drift through your mind."

Mira envisioned it. The sky was golden with the setting sun, the clouds tinged with violet.

"The clouds are not the sky," the monk continued, "They come, they go, but the sky remains. Just like thoughts come and go, yet you remain. And perhaps, as you notice that now, you begin to feel a sense of expansion, of openness, of something within you that has always been free."

Jian felt his chest expand. It was strange—how something so simple could feel so... true.

"And as you breathe, you may start to notice that this feeling of space is growing within you, that you, too, are vast and boundless, untouched by the passing of thoughts and emotions. And as you realize this, you can feel that deep peace settling into every part of you."

Section Three: The Mirror of the Self

"Now," the monk's voice softened, "imagine a great mirror before you. In it, you see yourself. The name you answer to, the body you inhabit, the story you tell about who you are."

Mira's reflection stared back at her. Strong. Determined. But was that all?

"Now step back," the monk instructed. "The reflection is not you. The mirror holds an image, but you are the one looking. You are not the story. You are the storyteller. You are the awareness, and because you are the awareness, you are free."

Jian blinked. He had always been Jian—the careful, logical one. But now, a part of him wondered. If he was not the story, then who was he?

Master Rohan let the silence linger, allowing the realization to settle like soft rain.

Section Four: The Dance of Awareness

"You are both the wave and the ocean," Master Rohan continued, his voice warm like the glow of temple lanterns. "Both the character and the consciousness. The form and the formless."

Mira's breath slowed. It was as though something ancient within her recognized these words. Like remembering something she had always known.

"And when you know this..." the monk's smile was almost mischievous, "you dance through life like a river flowing, like a cloud drifting, like the Buddha smiling beneath the Bodhi tree."

Jian chuckled. "So... life is a dance?"

Master Rohan nodded. "A beautiful, flowing dance of consciousness. And as you move through your day, you may begin to notice moments where this truth reveals itself to you, naturally, effortlessly. And when it does, you might find yourself smiling."

Guided Meditation: Returning as the Eternal Consciousness

"Now, slowly, return to the body," he instructed. "But not as before. Return knowing that you are both the actor and the observer. The dreamer and the dream."

One by one, the students opened their eyes.

Ravi saw the temple anew. The walls, the incense curling into the air, the gentle light pooling on the floor. Everything shimmered with presence.

Mira inhaled deeply. The colors seemed richer. The sounds clearer. Was this what it meant to truly see?

Affirmations

Master Rohan stood and spread his arms wide. "Repeat these words in your heart, as if planting them deep into the soil of your being."

"I am not my story. I am the awareness in which all stories arise."

"I am the infinite sky, vast and untouched, beyond all limitations."

The students breathed them in like air, letting them settle deep into their souls.

Conclusion

Master Rohan looked at each of them, his eyes twinkling. "Remember this, my dear students—when you feel lost, step back. When you feel small, look up. When you forget who you are, watch the river flow."

The sun had dipped low in the sky, painting the temple in hues of gold and crimson.

"You are the vastness. You are the awareness. And life? Life is the dance of the Buddha within you."

A deep stillness settled over the students, not of silence, but of understanding.

Questions for Further Discussion

1. How does the metaphor of the river help us understand the impermanence of identity?
2. In what ways do we hold onto our "story," and how can we learn to release it?
3. How does seeing ourselves as the infinite sky change how we handle our emotions?
4. What does it mean to be both the wave and the ocean? How does this perspective shift our daily experiences?
5. How can stepping back from our own self-image help us find more clarity in life?
6. What daily practices can we use to reinforce the awareness of being the observer rather than the story?
7. How does realizing we are not our thoughts change the way we interact with the world?

Dancing Buddha's Quote

"A cloud never fears dissolving, for it knows it was always the sky. You, too, need not fear change, for you are the awareness in which all things arise and fade."

CONCLUSION

THE JOURNEY FORWARD: EMBRACING THE DANCE

As we come to the end of this book, we find ourselves not at a conclusion, but at a beginning. The stories and meditations shared here were not meant to lead you to a final answer, but to open doors—doorways to awareness, to healing, and to your infinite capacity for growth and love. They were offered as lanterns, lighting the path as you walk forward into your own journey.

And even now, as you read these words, you may begin to notice a gentle awareness rising within you. Perhaps it's a sense of clarity, a quiet recognition that something within you is shifting. Or maybe it's just a subtle curiosity, wondering how the lessons you've absorbed will continue to reveal themselves in your life. Either way, you are here, in this moment, and that is enough.

Much like the Dancing Buddha, life calls us to move with grace and fluidity. There will be moments of stillness and moments of movement, times to leap and times to rest. And even as you consider these words, you might begin to imagine yourself moving through life with a sense of ease, a natural rhythm emerging, as if you've always known this dance.

Carrying the Lessons Forward
Living the Stories

The monk and student stories you've explored are not relics of an ancient past. They are reflections of your life—your struggles, your joys, your doubts, and your discoveries. Each character, whether it was the curious student, the wise monk, or the symbols woven into their lessons, represents an aspect of yourself.

Take a moment now and allow yourself to step outside of yourself for a moment—as if you were an observer watching your own journey unfold. As you do, notice what you see. Perhaps you recognize the student within, that part of you that longs to learn, to grow, to question. Or maybe you sense the monk within, the steady presence of wisdom that has always been there, waiting patiently to be heard. And as you shift between these perspectives, you might realize that you are both the student and the monk, the seeker and the guide.

The Student Within: Carry the spirit of curiosity and humility. Be willing to ask questions, to listen deeply, and to embrace not knowing as part of the journey. Growth begins with the courage to explore.

The Monk Within: Cultivate wisdom and compassion. Each step you take is an opportunity to respond to life's challenges with presence and kindness, both toward yourself and others.

And as you think about the stories you've encountered, you may find yourself recalling a particular lesson that resonates deeply. Perhaps it's the image of the kite caught in the wires, or the flame in the chamber, or the struggling tree reaching toward the sun. And just for a moment, imagine carrying that lesson forward into your life. Feel it settling into your mind, your heart, your being.

Practicing the Meditations

The guided meditations are tools for transformation. They are not just practices for the moments you sit in stillness but guides for how you walk through the world.

Inner Peace: Breathe deeply when the chaos of life begins to pull you away from yourself. Let the flame of your heart steady you, a constant light amidst the winds of change.

Resilience: Embrace your emotions as the river embraces each leaf. Let them flow, knowing they are transient and do not define you.

Unconditional Love: Hold love in your heart as freely as the rain falls. Let it nourish you and those around you without conditions or demands.

Letting Go: Step out of the shadows of the past and into the light of the present. Release what no longer serves you, trusting in the renewal that follows.

Purpose: Walk forward with the clarity of your inner flame, trusting it to guide you toward your truest self.

And as you consider these meditations, you might begin to notice how naturally they align with the rhythm of your own life. As if they've always been there, waiting for you to recognize them.

The Dance of the Buddha

The Dancing Buddha is more than a symbol. It is an invitation to see life as a rhythm—one that includes joy and sorrow, expansion and contraction, movement and stillness. To dance with life is to embrace its wholeness, to move with its changing tempo without resistance.

And even now, as you read these words, you can begin to feel a gentle sense of flow emerging within you. Like a soft current beneath the surface, guiding you effortlessly forward. You don't have to force it, you don't even have to try. Just allow yourself to follow where it leads, knowing that wherever you are, you are exactly where you need to be.

A Final Meditation: The Light of the Journey

Take a moment now to sit comfortably, allowing your body to relax. Let your eyes close gently and take a deep breath in... and exhale slowly. Another deep breath, filling your body with calm... and release, letting go of any tension. One more deep breath, and as you exhale, feel yourself settling into stillness.

Now, imagine yourself standing at the edge of a vast horizon. Before you is an open path, illuminated by soft, golden light. This path represents your journey—your unique steps forward, carrying all the lessons and wisdom you've gathered.

Notice a gentle light glowing in your chest. This is the light of your inner flame, steady and warm. With every breath, feel it grow brighter, its warmth spreading through your entire body. This light represents your clarity, your love, and your connection to purpose.

Now imagine this light radiating outward, illuminating the path ahead. As it shines, you see the steps of your journey clearly—each one an opportunity to grow, to heal, and to give. Feel the calm of knowing that this light will always guide you, no matter where the path leads.

Take a moment to stand in this glow, feeling the strength and clarity within you. With each breath, affirm to yourself:

> *I carry the light of wisdom and love within me, guiding my path forward.*

> *I am balanced, resilient, and ready to embrace the journey ahead.*

When you're ready, imagine yourself stepping forward onto the path, knowing you are supported by the lessons you've learned and the light you carry.

Take a deep breath in... and release. Slowly bring your awareness back to the present, opening your eyes when you're ready.

Moving Forward

As you close this book, take with you the understanding that you are always a student and a teacher, a seeker and a guide. Life will continue to present you with opportunities to grow, to heal, and to love. With the stories and practices you've explored here, you are more prepared than ever to step forward with grace and courage.

This journey is yours, but you are never alone. The wisdom of the Dancing Buddha, the monk and student, and the light within you will always be there to guide your way.

Final Words

Each moment, each breath, offers a chance to begin again. Take these lessons not as answers but as companions on your journey. Dance with life, trust your light, and know that wherever you are, you are exactly where you need to be.

Reaching Out – Healing Stories of the Dancing Buddha

Gregory K. Cadotte

ABOUT THE AUTHOR

Gregory K. Cadotte is a Certified Clinical Hypnotist, a Certified Clinical Hypnotherapist, and accredited NLP Master Practitioner dedicated to guiding others toward self-discovery, transformation, and personal mastery. With a deep interest and understanding of hypnosis, Neuro-Linguistic Programming (NLP), and consciousness exploration, Gregory integrates both science and spirituality to help individuals unlock their potential.

EXPLORE THE POWER OF ZOOM HYPNOTHERAPY AT LIGHT MANOR HYPNOTHERAPY

If the stories and meditations in *Reaching Out* have resonated with you, consider taking the next step in your journey toward healing and transformation. At **Light Manor Hypnotherapy**, we offer compassionate, client-centered sessions designed to help you overcome habits, release past burdens, and step into a life of clarity and well-being. Through a unique **donation-based model**, we make hypnotherapy accessible to all, ensuring that support is available regardless of financial circumstances. Whether you seek relief, renewal, or a deeper connection with yourself, we invite you to experience the profound benefits of hypnotherapy. Learn more or book a session at **www.light-manor.ca**.

Gregory K. Cadotte

www.ingramcontent.com/pod-product-compliance
Lightning Source LLC
Chambersburg PA
CBHW070529010526
44118CB00012B/1083